HAUNTED ARIZONA

GHOSTS OF THE GRAND CANYON STATE

Ellen Robson

AMERICAN
TRAVELER PRESS

Cover art by Kris Steele

DEDICATION
This book is lovingly dedicated to Rebeca,
Steven, Logan, Maddie and Griffin.

Photos of Winged Statues at Hoover Dam (page 48) courtesy U. S. Department of the Interior—Bureau of Reclamation. Photo by: Andrew Pernick

Library of Congress Cataloging-in-Publication Data
Robson, Ellen, 1946—
Haunted Arizona: Ghosts of the Grand Canyon State / by Ellen Robson.
    p. cm.
Includes bibliographical references; Index
ISBN 1-885590-90-3 (perfect bound)
1. Ghosts—Arizona. 2. Haunted Places—Arizona. I. Title
BF1472.U6 R647 2002
133.1'09791—dc21

                            2002008917

Printed in the United States of America

ISBN 13: #978-1-885590-90-9
ISBN 10: #1-885590-90-3

2012 printing

Information in this book is deemed to be authentic and accurate by author and publisher. However, they disclaim any liability incurred in connection with the use of information appearing in this book.

American Traveler Press
5738 North Central Avenue
Phoenix, AZ 85012
800-521-9221
www.AmericanTravelerPress.com

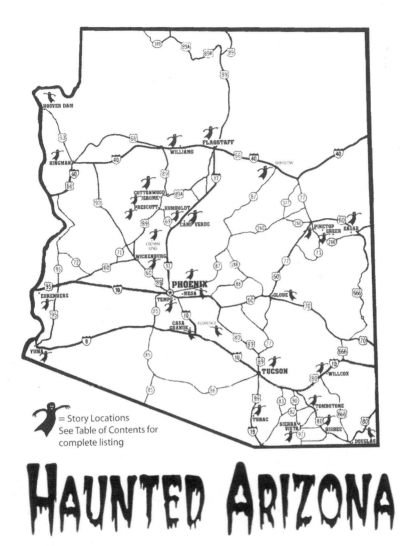

= Story Locations
See Table of Contents for
complete listing

HAUNTED ARIZONA

GHOSTS OF THE GRAND CANYON STATE

Beware!

At the time this book went to press all the listed locations were open to the public. As businesses come and go and hours of operation change, readers are advised to phone ahead when planning to visit. Contact each area's chamber of commerce for additional travel and lodging information (see page 128).

TABLE OF CONTENTS

Introduction.. 7

BISBEE

INN AT CASTLE ROCK—*Can an Old Miner "Return to Paradise?"* 9

CAMP VERDE

FORT VERDE STATE HISTORIC PARK—
Is Someone A.W.O.L. Here? 12

CASA GRANDE

CASA GRANDE CAFÉ—*Has the Spirit Been Exorcised?*.............. 14

THE PROPERTY CONFERENCE CENTER—
The Grande Lady in White 16

COTTONWOOD

COTTONWOOD HOTEL—
Hell Hath No Fury Like a Spirit Scorned!..................... 18

CROWN KING

CROWN KING SALOON & RESTAURANT—
They Serve Wine and Spirits at this Party!..................... 21

DOUGLAS

GADSDEN HOTEL—*The Ghost Who Lost His Head*............... 23

EAGAR

4th Avenue's VINTAGE HIDEAWAY—*Genieva's Conventions* 25

EHRENBERG

EHRENBERG CEMETERY—*Six Feet Under...or Not?*............. 28

FLAGSTAFF

CAFÉ ESPRESS—*The Voices Always Sound So Happy!* 30

CRYSTAL MAGIC—*Cellar Dwellers* 32

HOTEL WEATHERFORD—*Heartbreak Hotel?* 34

FLORENCE

TAYLOR'S BED & BREAKFAST—*Who's Been Sleeping in My Bed?* ... 36

GLOBE

COBRE VALLEY CENTER FOR THE ARTS—
Theater of the Condemned................................. 38

OLD GILA COUNTY JAIL—*Dead Woman Walking*.............. 42

JOHNNY'S COUNTRY CORNER—*A Lonesome Cowboy?*.......... 44

GREER

WHITE MOUNTAIN LODGE—*A Real 'Whodunit'* 46

HOOVER DAM

HOOVER DAM—*A Few 'Dammed' Souls* 48

HUMBOLDT

RIATA PASS GALLERY—*A Pause for Reflection* 51

JEROME

CONNOR HOTEL—*Re-living in the Lap of Luxury* 54

THE HAUNTED HAMBURGER—*If I Had a Hammer* 57

KINGMAN

HOTEL BRUNSWICK—*Three Ghosts Find Rooms* 59

MESA

THE LANDMARK RESTAURANT—
Paranormal Seems to Be the Norm Here! 62

PHOENIX

AUNT CHILADA'S AT SQUAW PEAK—
At This Bar, They Did Serve Miners! 64

PIONEER ARIZONA LIVING HISTORY MUSEUM—
Phantoms of the Opera House 67

HOTEL SAN CARLOS—*The Pitter-Patter of Little Ghostly Feats* 69

TEETER HOUSE—*Lady Ghosts Get Tea'd Off!* 71

VALLEY YOUTH THEATRE—*A British Invasion* 73

PINETOP

CHARLIE CLARK'S STEAKHOUSE—*Does Charlie Still Stop By?* 76

PRESCOTT

COYOTE JOE'S BAR AND GRILL—*A Real Working Girl's Ghost* 78

HASSAYAMPA INN—*He Left Her On Their Wedding Night!* 80

PRESCOTT FINE ARTS ASSOCIATION—
The Case of the Missing Corpse 82

SIERRA VISTA

DAISY MAE'S STRONGHOLD—*Ghost Host With the Most* 84

TEMPE

CASEY MOORE'S OYSTER HOUSE—*The Ballroom Dancer* 86

MONTI'S LA CASA VIEJA—
This 'Old House' is Filled With Fine Spirits! 88

TOMBSTONE

    NELLIE CASHMAN'S RESTAURANT—*An Angel Among Us* 92

    TOMBSTONE BOARDING HOUSE—*The Not-So O.K. Corral* 94

TUBAC

    TUBAC GOLF RESORT—
        When Johnny Comes Marching Home Again. 96

TUCSON

    HOTEL CONGRESS—*A Crime Story and a Ghost Tale* 98

    LI'L ABNER'S STEAKHOUSE—*Things Go Better with Coca-Cola!* . . 100

    UNIVERSITY OF ARIZONA'S CENTENNIAL HALL—
        The Man in Black. 102

VAIL

    COLOSSAL CAVE—*A Spelunking Spirit!.* 104

WICKENBURG

    VULTURE CITY—*A Heavy 'Lode' for These Ghosts!* 107

WILLCOX

    FARAWAY RANCH—*This Ghost Shakes...and Bakes!.* 110

    REX ALLEN MUSEUM and WILLCOX COWBOY
        HALL OF FAME—*This Cowboy Just Can't Stop Singin'!.* 112

WILLIAMS

    THE RED GARTER BED & BAKERY—*Prostitute or Poltergeist?* 114

    ROD'S STEAK HOUSE—*Rodney's Danger Field.* 117

    WILLIAMS DEPOT—
        Have Your (Harvey) Girl Call My (Harvey) Girl! 119

WINSLOW

    BO JO'S GRILL & SPORTS CLUB—
        Don't Be Afraid...It's Only 'Grandpa'!. 121

    RIALTO THEATER—*Theater of the Absurd!* 123

YUMA

    YUMA TERRITORIAL PRISON—
        Desperadoes, Why Don't You Come to Your Senses? 125

Bibliography, Books, Articles, Videos. 127
About the Author 129
Acknowledgments. 129
Index. 130

INTRODUCTION

A cold touch brushes against your arm ever so lightly...an old miner tweaks your toes...an uninvited presence "crawls" into bed with you. Ghosts, at least most of the ghosts in the Grand Canyon State, are fun-loving and a bit on the pesky side, but the owners and managers of the restaurants, hotels and gift shops in this book all agree on one thing: Ghosts are a part of the family lore and are welcome to stay.

Arizona's past is rich with tales of the Wild West, and the proprietors and caretakers in *Haunted Arizona* swear that the spirits who lived that history are still among us. From ruthless outlaws and benign bandits, to priests and Victorian ladies, *Haunted Arizona* will introduce you to a variety of these ghosts—as different from each other as the locations in which they once dwelled.

When I started writing *Haunted Arizona*, my intention was to flush out one ghost story per town. I soon realized it wasn't going to be quite that simple. For one thing, some towns had nary a scary tale. Payson, for example, where legend has it that a local sheriff would chain drunk men to a tree until they sobered up enough to ride back to their ranches, didn't produce a hint of a ghost. Likewise, Peoria and Glendale—not a ghost in sight.

On the other end of the spectrum, however, when I explored Prescott, the state's first capital, I had to leave some ghost stories behind. It was difficult to decide which ones to keep but I think you'll be happy with my choices. You can plan an entire day around three haunted locations there. Start off by enjoying a scrumptious meal at Coyote Joe's; then catch a live performance at the Prescott Fine Arts Association, where the body of a Roman Catholic Priest disappeared, back when it was Sacred Heart Church. Next, spend the night at the Hassayampa Inn. But be careful: You may wake up in the middle of the night when "Faith," the unhappy wife who committed suicide there, turns on your radio, or the "Night Watchman" rattles your doors and windows.

In Phoenix, I had to stop at five stories, although I know of many more. Even small communities, such as Casa Grande, Williams and Globe produced two or more accounts in their spirit-rich towns.

Ehrenberg, population of about 2,000, came through with a cemetery that has been haunted since 1908, according to the late author Martha Summerhayes.

How did I uncover these ghosts? Some stories came about through old newspaper articles and other media sources or from the Internet. Other stories I stumbled upon while doing research for another story. Friends and family assisted, too.

One day, on a whim, I stopped by Fat Cat Cookies in Phoenix because it was located in an old building. I explained to the owner that I was writing *Haunted Arizona* and would love to include her business if she had any ghosts. Although Linda didn't have any in that bakery, she gave me a delightful account of the two late-19th-century Victorian ladies who had "visited" her at her old location. Also in Phoenix, The Hotel San Carlos, famous for its spirits—Leone Jensen and three rambunctious little boy ghosts, deserved to be included as well. And, I just couldn't leave out Arizona's most famous haunted hotel, the Gadsden in Douglas.

All the sites have recurring themes: unexplained noises, objects moved to different spots, doors opening and shutting, faucets turned on, and, yes, sometimes even ghostly apparitions. And finally, everyone seems to agree that ghosts get agitated and more active when changes occur on a site—such as building renovations or simply the presence of a new owner.

Haunted Arizona is a travel guide for those who want to gain a fascinating insight into the history and legends of the places they visit. Visitors are welcome at all the sites, so embark on a journey and explore the haunted side of Arizona!

Ellen Robson

BISBEE

INN AT CASTLE ROCK

CAN AN OLD MINER
"RETURN TO PARADISE?"

Visitors are enticed to Bisbee, a romantic town nestled in the Mule Mountains, for its old-world charm. Ghosts are enticed to the Inn at Castle Rock because the accommodations are, quite literally, out of this world.

The bed and breakfast, built in 1890, started out as a miner's boarding house. Today, an original mineshaft, located in the dining room of this three-story, eye-catching Victorian wonder, has been converted into a spring-fed well. While enjoying their meal, guests are entertained by koi (creatures resembling colossal goldfish) swimming in the well.

Return to Paradise Room

With all of the renovations that have taken place over the years, it's no wonder that many of the Inn's former "inhabitants" should make their presence known. From time to time, in fact, some of them have nearly worn out their welcome.

An old miner, for example, who no doubt roomed here as a regular at the turn of the 19th century, is satisfied to stay put in the Inn's "Return to Paradise" room. If you choose to sleep in the single bed instead of the double, don't be surprised if you feel someone tweaking your toes during the night. Legend has it that it's just the harmless ghost of the old miner, wondering when he'll get his private room back and "return" to "paradise."

*The Inn
at Castle Rock*

One guest who stayed in the White Eagle room mentioned that her orange cat was unusually inquisitive about the miner's old room, which was directly across the hall. "Morris was fascinated with this room," Jennifer Baker explained. "He wasn't the least bit afraid though. Whenever he was in the hallway and the door was shut, he kept trying to look under the door meowing, and when the door happened to be opened, he would poke his head in and look all around."

Baker didn't let Morris roam freely through the bed and breakfast, but from time to time, he did manage to escape. Once he was on the loose, he would high-tail it straight across the hall to the Return to Paradise room. One afternoon Morris scampered off with Jennifer in tow. The cat was too fast and dived under the single bed, scooting to the back. No amount of coaxing or pleading worked; he was determined to stay under that bed. Finally, the innkeeper managed to grab Morris and carried him back to Baker's room, the cat kicking and screeching all the way.

Knowing that animals have an uncanny sense for the unknown, Baker couldn't help but wonder if what Morris sensed in that room might have followed them back to their room.

She found out on New Year's Eve 2000.

Baker had decided to take a catnap before going out on the town. Her room was dim but not totally dark, and she was in a quasi-sleep stage, when all of a sudden, a shimmering light appeared a foot or two above her bed. She thought at first some type of film over her eyes was causing the cloudy illusion. But after a few good blinks, Baker's apparition didn't disappear. "It was the size of a person except it was more of an oblong shape, floating, very distinct and vague," Baker said. "It was just hovering and glistening and eventually disappeared. But, for some reason, I wasn't the least bit frightened."

Another time, Robert Stroub, a guest on the second floor, was startled by a shadow that passed eerily in front of him in the hallway. Stroub, who doesn't believe in ghosts, could offer no explanation. A female ghost, dressed in Victorian garb, has been known to walk up and down the stairs, so perhaps it was her silhouette that crossed his path.

Two employees have also had encounters with ghosts at the inn. Maintenance man Robert "Bert" Visor has seen two women, both dressed in old-fashioned attire, and Christine Rodriguez, another employee, got a passing glance of a small boy.

Stairway to the second floor

Jeannene Babcock, owner of the Inn at Castle Rock, is content with her family of ghosts, whom she says are "benign and fairly good." Lights go on and off and employees and guests alike have experienced cold spots from time to time. A psychic once told Babcock that "protective spirits" were watching over her inn. Babcock says she knows for sure that one of them is her father who took an old miners' boarding house and turned it into a charming and lore-filled bed and breakfast.

Address:	Inn at Castle Rock
	112 Tombstone Canyon Road
	Bisbee, AZ 85603
Phone:	(800) 566-4449
Website:	www.theinn.org

Directions: From Phoenix: Take I-10 East to Tucson then continue on I-10 east to Exit 303 at Benson. Follow SR80 south to Bisbee. Take Downtown Bisbee Exit to the first stop sign and turn left onto Main which becomes Tombstone Canyon Road. Inn at Castle Rock is on your left.

FORT VERDE STATE HISTORIC PARK

IS SOMEONE A.W.O.L. HERE?

Camp Verde, renamed Fort Verde in 1879, was abandoned in 1891.

According to Bob Munson, a previous manager of Fort Verde State Historic Park, you have to take the reports of ghostly activity at this old Army post with a grain of salt.

Construction of Camp Verde began in 1871 and was used by the Army patrols mainly as a supply post and staging area. In all, 22 buildings were erected to house two companies of cavalry and two of infantry. Camp Verde, renamed to Fort Verde in 1879, was abandoned in 1891 to the Department of the Interior.

The administrative office and a museum are housed in what had been staff headquarters. The remaining 3 buildings house the Commanding Officer's Quarters, the Surgeon's Quarters and the Bachelor Officer's Quarters. Each is a unique museum that reflects the lifestyles of their occupants.

The main museum will be your first stop, but a word of warning. Be prepared for heavy footsteps interrupting any conversation you may be having when you're in the hallway. But don't blame a staff member or another visitor for the annoying disturbance. And it won't do you any good to track down the clunking sound. Munson and other members of the staff have already done that and the hallway is always bare, of humans that is. Could this be the spirit of an officer once stationed at the old fort still on duty?

The other ghost is a puzzle to everyone; a pretty young Victorian woman who wears period night clothing. The few people who have seen her apparition always describe her as looking very distressed.

Apparently she has made herself at home on the second floor of the Commanding Officer's Quarters, as this is where quite a bit of activity happens. In 1999, after touring Officers' Row, a female visitor descending the stairway experienced an ever so light brush against her arm. She was not at all pleased with the occurrence. Another accused a ghost of pushing her son down the same stairway. Still others report seeing a female ghost, garbed in white, on the upstairs landing. There has also been speculation that, late at night, candles can be seen flickering through the windows on the second floor.

The staff members aren't exactly sure who this unhappy ghost is. Before it was abandoned to the Department of the Interior, the fort allowed only four enlisted men to bring their wives with them, but since she is seen in the Commanding Officer's quarters she most likely was an officer's wife.

Munson points out that only one tragic death occurred at the old cavalry fort, and that happened when two buddies were horsing around and one of their guns accidentally went off, killing the other.

Be alert in the Commanding Officer's Quarters—there's a very unhappy woman here who doesn't stand at ease!

Address: Fort Verde State Historic Park
                    125 E. Hollamon
                    Camp Verde, AZ 86322

Phone: (928) 567-3275

Hours: 8 a.m.-5 p.m., daily except for Christmas

Directions: From Phoenix: Take I-17 North to Exit 285 (General Crook Road). Travel east for 2 miles, turn left on Main street and go 2 blocks to Hollamon. Turn right, the Park is on your right.

CASA
GRANDE

CASA GRANDE CAFÉ

HAS THE SPIRIT BEEN EXORCISED?

Historic atmosphere, excellent food and a variety of ghosts are what you'll find at the Casa Grande Café. Considering the history of the building, it's no wonder there is such a hodgepodge of spirits. Since 1907, this small adobe structure has been home to many different proprietors.

It started out as Johnson's Grocery Store. The owner's untimely death happened a few years later when he was gunned down in front of his store by *banditos*. The outlaws were ultimately hung for their crime.

Is this Mr. Johnson's booth?

Is the old man who has been seen sitting in a booth from time to time the original owner, the murdered Mr. Johnson? He wears an outdated vest and sports old-fashioned muttonchops. No one knows, of course, but the sight of him has made many a waitress here forgo her tip.

From 1940 to 1955 this building was home to one of the first laundromats in the Casa Grande area. In 1960 the building housed a restaurant named Sophia's. The restaurant later became the Casa Grande Café and was purchased by Joe Revak in 1980.

"Most of the former restaurant help stayed on and they told me that every once in awhile a pan or pot would fly off a shelf and crash into the wall on the opposite side of the kitchen," advised Mr. Revak.

Then there's the spirit in the back room. Although no one has actually seen that ghost, employees say they feel cold chills and believe they advertise someone's ghostly presence.

"One instance that I was involved in happened when I was sitting in 'Mr. Johnson's Booth' holding my 1-year-old daughter," Revak related. "She suddenly stiffened up, convulsed and somersaulted right out of my arms onto the floor! She was not injured, but I became very angry because I felt something or someone was trying to take control of me."

"I called a pastor and he and his wife (also a pastor), came right over. They said they did not sense anything wrong with the area in which I had been sitting, but when they tried to enter the kitchen the pastor's wife experienced a choking sensation and could not continue. Her husband, however, was able to perform an exorcism. Afterwards, they both told me that there had been an evil spirit in the kitchen, but that it was now gone."

Wherever there are ghosts, there are strange occurrences and the Casa Grande Café is no exception. It is said that when staff walk through a specific area of the kitchen, they seem to blank out for an instant and lose all train of thought. Was the exorcism not thorough enough?

Maybe Mr. Johnson is not the only ghost here. Are the *banditos* who murdered Mr. Johnson "hanging around?" Or, perhaps one of the laundromat machines didn't give the right change and an irritated customer is still looking for his credit!

Address:	Casa Grande Café
	301 North Picacho
	Casa Grande, AZ 85222
Phone:	(520) 426-1424
Hours:	10 a.m.-2 p.m., daily
Note:	(New owners Enrique and Lupe Carrillo plan to rename the restaurant "Lupita's Mexican Food".)

Directions: From Phoenix: Take I-10 East to Exit 195 (SR84) turn west. Keep right at the fork and merge onto SR387, which becomes North Pinal Rd. and then West 2nd Street. Turn left at North Picacho St., the café is on your right—across from the Catholic Church.

CASA GRANDE

THE PROPERTY CONFERENCE CENTER

THE GRANDE LADY IN WHITE

The Property Conference Center

Glancing at this building on the outskirts of Casa Grande you would never suspect that the charming structure is home to the bizarre ghost of one of the original owners.

Peter Ethington and his wife had the 5,000-square-foot home built for their large family in the early 1940s. Considered at the time to be a mansion, the house sat on 16 sections of land.

When Michael Jackson (not the pop star) purchased the building more than 25 years ago, he was aware that it was a package deal: The Ethington's old house and the land—and the ghost of the late Mrs. Ethington, better known as "The Lady in White" because of her fondness for white clothing.

In 1979, an employee of Jackson's had an experience that not only drove him out of the building but out of the country. At the time, the worker was living in the basement and had seen a vision of The Lady in White on one of the walls. He was so frightened that he ran naked through the desert, trying to get away. His co-workers collected his last paycheck for him since the worker refused to go back on the property.

A few years later, just after closing, the bar manager was on the phone with Jackson when she heard her name called out twice. She knew she was the only one in the locked building. Closing alone was difficult enough, even without agitation from Mrs. Ethington.

Another 10-year employee later admitted the only time in his life that he was scared was when he had to lock up the conference center.

Fay Horton, a native of Casa Grande, has had a few run-ins with this ghost as well. Horton was married to The Lady in White's granddaughter, and while the two were courting, one time, he spent the night. Was he ever in for a surprise. He'd had his clothes at the foot of the bed, but the following morning had to go searching for them. Horton finally located them in another bedroom, folded tidily at the foot of that bed. He knew the late Mrs. Ethington was to be held accountable, as he was the only one in her former home that night.

The Lady in White made several appearances to Horton, and each time, an unmistakable odor preceded her manifestation. She even dropped in on him at his residence. One morning she appeared to him in front of his bed. "If you renounce Jesus, I will give you anything you want," she is alleged to have said. Considering that Peter Ethington and his wife were staunch Baptists, this remark startled Horton.

As with the former employee and Fay Horton, Jackson's own experience occurred in the basement, too. He was asleep when The Lady in White decided to visit. "I'm a very light sleeper and something woke me up," Jackson says. "I could feel a very heavy, heavy presence that seemed to be coming down the stairs. I wasn't afraid, as I knew she wouldn't harm me. She never did materialize—not even a shadow. But I could certainly feel her company."

You may never have occasion to attend a conference or a banquet at the Property Conference Center. But, you could always rent a room and bring out a Ouija board. Who knows? Maybe the planchette will be moved by The Lady in White!

Address:	The Property Conference Center
	1251 W. Gila Bend Highway
	Casa Grande, AZ 85222
Phone:	(520) 836-2045

Directions: From Phoenix: Take I-10 East; exit onto SR84, go west until SR84 turns into the Gila Bend Hwy. The Property Conference Center is on your left.

COTTONWOOD

COTTONWOOD HOTEL

HELL HATH NO FURY
LIKE A SPIRIT SCORNED!

The ghosts who refuse to leave the Cottonwood Hotel pretty much stay on the second floor. Who they are remains a mystery to owner Karen Leff. Because they choose not to be seen, even their gender is unknown. Leff has an inkling, though, that one of them just might be George Brooks.

The hotel, which is on the National Historic Register, is located in Old Town Cottonwood and is a self-catered bed and breakfast. Each of the five suites—the George H. Brooks, Elvis, Desert Fury, Mae West and John Wayne—has its own unique décor. But George Brooks isn't picky. He'll haunt any of the suites.

Here is Leff's explanation:

Brooks was a renowned psychic, spiritualist and Doctor of Divinity who was born in London, England. He lived in Los Angeles around the turn of the 19th century and frequented the Cottonwood Hotel, staying there whenever he came to the area to do lectures and workshops in the Verde Valley. In 1925, he predicted that Cottonwood would see its biggest catastrophe ever. The night after he made his

The Cottonwood Hotel

prediction, a large bootlegging still blew up and wiped out the whole west side of town. Oddly enough, Brooks was the only fatality. His skeletal remains were found in the rubble of the burnt structure of the original Cottonwood Hotel, far from where his room was located. Some said it looked as though he had been trying to escape the fire by running down the corridor away from it. Others surmised that he may have been murdered as he scared many with his predictions and they frowned upon his visits.

The present Cottonwood Hotel was rebuilt on the same site as the original structure, with rooms, stairways and corridors almost exactly matching the original building. Even today, unexplained footsteps are often heard in the corridors and have given some roomers chills. They explain that it is as if someone is trying to feel their way down the hallway. Is Brooks' spirit still trying to find a way out? Items also swing and drop from closets in the middle of the night, while pictures fall to the floor or mysteriously get turned upside down.

The Brooks Suite, which corresponds to the rooms he stayed in at the old hotel, is relatively quiet, though Leff says she once found a wall decoration turned upside down when the room had been vacant and locked for days.

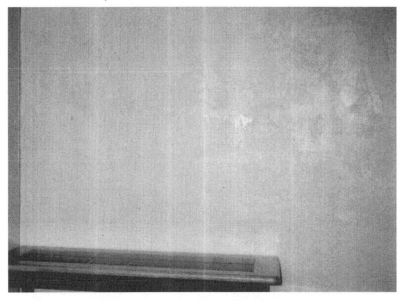

Is this a "spirit photograph" of the ghost? Note the images at the right.

Shortly after purchasing the hotel in 1996, Leff says she knew it was no ordinary inn. Once, during the renovation of the then-vacant Desert Fury Suite, sounds could be heard coming from inside. One couple mentioned that they could hear the door being shut, the bed squeaking and even the shower running. Leff thought how strange this was considering there wasn't a stick of furniture in the room. Now that the room is being rented out, the ghost keeps Leff busy elsewhere in the hotel picking up items from kitchen shelves that have been mysteriously scattered about the floor.

Leff was once lucky enough to acquire a "spirit photograph" of the ghost: Unexplained images on a wall appeared in two photos Leff had taken in the kitchen area of the Desert Fury Suite. One image showed a man with gray hair, sitting next to a female who was holding a flashlight. They were both glancing at a big book, and another image of a person behind them seemed to be engulfing the two of them.

Guests who are more attuned to the supernatural and have stayed in the John Wayne Suite have told Leff that they feel spirits moving around. One guest boarding in the room directly below the Desert Fury Suite asked recently who was staying upstairs and how much longer they planned on staying. The guest was taken aback when told the suite had been unoccupied for weeks.

If you stay in Cottonwood's oldest hotel, request the Desert Fury Suite and snap away. Who knows what might show up in your photographs?

Address:	Cottonwood Hotel 930 N. Main Street Cottonwood, AZ 86326
Phone:	(928) 634-9455
Website:	www.cottonwoodhotel.com

Directions: From Phoenix: Take I-17 North; exit at Camp Verde Exit (287). Turn left on SR260 to Cottonwood. Take 260 to 89A (S. Main St.). Go straight 3 miles. When South Main turns into North Main, go into Historic Old Town Cottonwood. The Cottonwood Hotel is on your left.

CROWN KING

CROWN KING SALOON & RESTAURANT

THEY SERVE WINE AND SPIRITS AT THIS PARTY!

As different as night and day, the ghosts who haunt the Crown King Saloon and Restaurant have no intention of leaving. And why should they? They have the run of the place, and the owners don't seem to mind a bit.

The Crown King Saloon, built in the 1880s, was originally located in Alexandria and moved to Oro Belle, a small mining camp five miles down the road. In 1906 the building was dismantled and hauled, piece-by-piece, by burro to Crown King.

Like so many other saloons and hotels in those days, the second floor was used as a brothel. Even then, however, "ladies of the night" were considered social outcasts, but "Leatherbelly" must have felt welcome—among both the living and the dead at the Crown King Saloon.

No one seems to remember why Leatherbelly was tagged with such an unusual name. As the "madam" she had her own room in the hotel (Room #7) and it is a well-known fact that she loved— and still loves—to party.

Crown King Saloon

Another ghost who appears from time to time is "Hugo," a Viet Nam veteran who also lived in Room #7. When employees "see" him, he is always wearing a long trench coat and a big broad-brimmed hat. Hugo is also a partier, just like his roommate, Leatherbelly.

Investigative work by the author revealed this tale from an anonymous source: "I was staying upstairs and could hear a party going on downstairs in the bar. I knew it was just Hugo and Leatherbelly, having a good time. Glasses were clinking and you could hear them laughing. They even provided their own music. And like so many other times, I heard them running up and down the hallway. When I get tired of their nonsense, I just tell them to go away and they usually obey me."

After surviving the rocky 26-mile drive on the dirt road that threads through the Bradshaw Mountains, you might want to rent out one of the rooms that sit above the saloon and restaurant. If you're lucky, maybe Hugo and Leatherbelly will invite you to a party!

Address:	Crown King Saloon & Restaurant 3 Main Street Crown King, AZ 86343
Phone:	(928) 632-7053
Hours:	Restaurant: Mon. thru Thurs.: 11 a.m.-5 p.m., Fri.: 11 a.m.-9 p.m. Sat.: 8 a.m.-9 p.m. Sun: 8 a.m.-6 p.m. Saloon: 10 a.m.-1 a.m., daily

Directions: From Phoenix: (This is a rough road. A four-wheel drive is recommended.) Take I-17 North; take Exit 248 and follow the signs to Crown King.

DOUGLAS

GADSDEN HOTEL

THE GHOST WHO LOST HIS HEAD!

Money was certainly no object when this five-story, 160-room structure was built in 1907. Since 1929, when the hotel was rebuilt after a disastrous fire, the Gadsden has been billed, "the last of the grand hotels." The ghosts who linger here must agree; they don't seem to be in any hurry to leave.

Looking down from the second floor at the elegant lobby, you think you've been transported to the early 1900s. As you descend the white Italian marble staircase you see four massive rose-colored faux marble columns that tower over the spacious foyer. Vaulted stained-glass skylights run the full length of the lobby and a Tiffany stained-glass mural extends across one wall of the massive mezzanine.

Lobby of the Gadsden Hotel

But don't let the tranquil atmosphere of this area of the hotel fool you. In October 2000, a security guard watched in trepidation as a ghost, dressed in black, sprinted across the lobby. Like all the other ghosts in this hotel, not much is known about his identity. Ghostly activity occurs from the basement to the fifth floor, and for some unknown reason, they seem to appear more during Lent and the Christmas season.

It was during the Lenten season in 1991 that hotel manager Robin Brekhus had an encounter with the most active ghost of the Gadsden. Brekhus was in the basement, looking for candles because of a power outage. In the beam of her flashlight, she saw a faceless figure shaped like a man. "He was dressed in fancy Western clothing," Brekhus says, "and came off like he might have been a gambler. The spirit just floated down the hallway."

A visiting psychic identified the ghost as "Jonathan."

Jonathan also paid a visit to Room 333 and, according to Brekhus, "crawled into bed with a female guest! I guess he was feeling amorous or maybe he just wanted to cuddle that night," she says. "The guest must have liked it, as she stayed an extra night and didn't request a different room."

Another ghost has been described as tall, headless, and clad in a cape and army-style khaki clothing. An elevator operator caught sight of this spirit once in the basement. When the operator saw him, he was wearing a shiny black suit, had very white hands but was still without a head!

On November 9, 1999, a cowboy in room 128 on the mezzanine level, couldn't figure out what was going on when he awoke in the middle of the night to find his bed and the lamps shaking violently. He thought he had survived an earthquake! No earthquake, of course, had been reported.

The hotel's ghosts aren't just of the male gender. A guest was in one of the women's restrooms by herself recently and when she looked in the mirror she saw the reflection of a woman sitting on the sofa. When the guest turned, no one was there.

While filming a movie on location at the Gadsden, actor Tom Selleck's head electrician had a frightening experience: While staying in Room 333, the electrician told management that he had seen lights flickering on and off. And, as if that weren't enough, he said, his golf bag had flown across his suite and the contents had gone everywhere.

A stay at the Gadsden Hotel is a must for those interested in headless ghosts. Just be sure to leave your golf bag at home!

Address:	The Gadsden Hotel
	1046 G. Avenue
	Douglas, AZ 85607
Phone:	(520) 364-4481 Website: www.gadsdenhotel.com

Directions: From Phoenix: Take I-10 East to Benson. Take SR80 through Tombstone and Bisbee to Douglas. SR80 becomes G Avenue when you enter Douglas. The Gadsden is on the right.

EAGAR

4th Avenue's
VINTAGE HIDEAWAY

GENIEVA'S CONVENTIONS

The Vintage Hideaway dates back to the 1930s when it served Eagar as a boarding house. Hank and Bessie Brawley began construction of Brawley Boarding House in 1925, and the unfinished house was later sold to Genieva and Milford (Mitt) Wiltbank. The Wiltbanks also took in renters, as did the Lou Gastineau family, who were the next owners. Lou sold the house to Daniel and Romelle Richard, who converted the boarding house into today's Vintage Hideaway.

Are Genieva and Mitt still here?

Two ghosts, Genieva, and the other (possibly her husband), had free rein of the building that sat empty for 10 years before the Richards purchased it in 1996. Instead of leaving to take refuge in another quiet abandoned structure, the ghosts decided to stay put.

"Aunt Genieva," as the staff fondly call her, is content to drop little hints to draw attention. She leaves the faucets dripping and, after business hours, she's known to flip the lights on and off. One of her favorite games is to tease the waitresses by rocking their water pitchers back and forth as they sit on the counters.

"Our ghost just likes to help keep an eye on things and very rarely scares anyone," Romelle says. "Her favorite places are the waitress station and our storeroom. Not only do we hear her footsteps, but the storeroom door that goes out into the hall opens or closes itself at times. There are no drafts in that area of the house."

The rooms upstairs are filled to the rafters with antiques, knick-knacks and, it seems, Aunt Genieva. The general consensus at the Vintage Hideaway is that their female ghost lives upstairs and only ventures down when she's in the mood to cause mischief. The waitresses can hear her shuffling about as she moves items off the shelves and scatters them on the floor.

Aunt Genieva's room

There are those among the employees, however, who do not believe in ghosts, and one of the cooks fit into that category. The cook "kept making comments about her existence until Genieva had had enough," Romelle says, laughing. "One time he was holding a large glass measuring cup full of pudding, and it shattered in his hand. The pudding was cold so the cook couldn't blame the incident on heat causing the explosion." Genieva had made her point: "The cook's a believer now," Romelle says.

Light footsteps, maybe from two or even three small children, can also be heard coming from the upstairs hall. There were quite a few Wiltbank children, but they are all alive, so Romelle says she isn't sure who those tiny footsteps belong to.

Romelle thinks the male ghost is

The upstairs hall

Genieva's husband, Mitt. "We've only seen him twice," she says. "When we first opened, we had a small bakery, and on occasion we would get customers very early in the morning. They would just walk in and, nine times out of 10, they would startle me. One morning I looked up and there was this guy standing there, just inside the door. I let him know right away that I had some donuts ready but hadn't had a chance to put them in the display case. When I returned with some, he had disappeared. I remember he was big and burly and wearing a red flannel shirt."

A few days after this incident, two psychics were having lunch at the Vintage Hideaway and one of them asked their waitress if she was aware that there was a ghost on the premises. The second psychic added that they actually had two ghosts, a male and a female. Romelle then realized that her early customer had actually been their second ghost!

The second time Mitt was seen, he was once again mistaken for a customer. One of the waitresses was passing through the dining room when she saw a man sitting alone at a table. When she returned from the waitress station, the chair was empty.

The Vintage Hideaway always closes for two and a half months during the winter, so this gives Aunt Genieva and Mitt the quiet they were used to before their home became a bustling restaurant. Romelle always hopes their ghosts will be there to greet them when they reopen every spring.

Address:	4th Avenue's Vintage Hideaway
	389 N. Eagar Street
	Eagar, AZ 85925
Phone:	(928) 333-4398
Hours:	10:30 a.m.-9:00 p.m. Monday-Saturday
	Closed Sunday

Directions: From Phoenix: Go northeast via SR87 through Payson; take SR260 to Show Low. Continue east on US60 to Springerville, then turn south on SR81 to Eagar. Turn left on Eagar Street, Vintage Hideaway is on your right. An alternate route is to go through Globe via US60 to Show Low and then to Eagar.

EHRENBERG

EHRENBERG CEMETERY

SIX FEET UNDER...OR NOT?

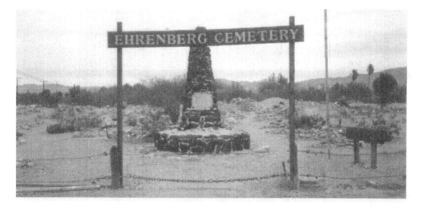

A scene straight from *Night of the Living Dead*: a moonless night, an old cemetery and dead people rising from their graves. That's exactly the scene in the Ehrenberg Cemetery, according to Martha Summerhayes, author of *Vanished Arizona* (originally published in 1908):

> *"The place was but a stone's throw for us, and the uneasy spirits from these desecrated graves began to haunt me. I could not sit alone on the porch at night, for they peered through the lattice, and mocked at me, and beckoned. Some had no hands, some no arms, but they pointed or nodded toward the gruesome burying-ground: 'You'll be with us soon, you'll be with us soon.'"*

Ehrenberg resident Vicki Green can relate. She may not have encountered a ghost with no head or arms wandering about (yet), but she knows firsthand how unearthly this place is after dark.

"A few days ago, my mother and I were here after the sun went down," Green said during a recent tour of the old cemetery. "When we were at one of the gravesites, we noticed some old charred wood and ashes on top. As we wondered out loud if it was the result of a small bonfire, a very powerful, strong stench seemed to engulf us. There isn't anything in the area that would cause a foul odor like that. It was almost as if someone or something wanted us to leave, and they succeeded! We couldn't get out of there fast enough. By the time we reached the car, which was just outside the fence, the rank smell had vanished altogether."

Green and a friend tried their hand at spirit photography at the cemetery. They arrived late at night, but this time Vicki stayed on the outside of the fence, sending her friend into the small graveyard. He pointed out various places where he felt strong energy while Vicki snapped away. They weren't disappointed. A few photos had luminescent balls of light that seemed to hover over the graves. The

Ghostly orbs

film also captured an image of a large amount of spirit energy starting from the ground, continuing upward and then veering to the right.

The sleepy town of Ehrenberg seems to be full of ghostly activity. Megan, Green's daughter, was once spending the night with her in her home on the opposite side of town from the cemetery. She spotted the ghost of a little girl darting back and forth and hiding around the corner of a building nearby. From the clothing she was wearing, Megan said, it appeared that she was from the old Gold Rush days. The child, clutching her doll, had looked extremely pale and later appeared to Megan in a dream. Megan said that she had the impression that the little girl's mother may have killed her because she was so sickly.

If you enter the Ehrenberg Cemetery keep in mind what Martha Summerhayes wrote: "…'You'll be with us soon, you'll be with us soon….' "

Address: Ehrenberg Cemetery
             Ehrenberg, AZ 85334

Directions: From Phoenix: Take I-10 West to just before the California border; take Exit 1 heading north. Turn left on Poston-Parker Road. The Ehrenberg Cemetery is on the left.

FLAGSTAFF

CAFÉ ESPRESS

THE VOICES ALWAYS SOUND SO HAPPY!

The history of this structure is vague, but the ghosts here are easily discerned. Owner Cathy Ryan says the building started out as the Flagstaff Theatre in 1918. In the 1950s it was converted to a woman's clothing store and, finally, in 1983 the Café Espress took its place.

"I knew all along that I had some occupants that were ghosts," Ryan says, "but since I was assured they weren't harmful, it didn't concern me. There are two, and they are quite playful. I've never seen them but I can sense their presence and can hear them. They come out at night when all is quiet, and I constantly hear muffled conversations coming from the catwalk

Happy ghosts at the Cafe Espress?

above the kitchen. The voices always sound so happy. I have also heard knocking."

Ryan's employees don't like to be in the building alone late at night because of those voices, but Cathy is used to them. Still, she finds herself going outside and around the restaurant to make sure the conversations are not human.

The previous owner, Stephen Herndon, opened up the Café Espress in 1983 and he, too, noticed ghostly activity.

Herndon and his wife did the build-out on the building, working long hours into the night. When Steve first heard the pounding noise, he went next door to try to track down the source. He finally determined the sounds were coming from the basement.

As soon as Herndon would go down the stairs, the pounding would quit. He kept on, though, and the farther into the basement Herndon would go, the more intensely he could feel some kind of presence. Once that happened, he says, he always declined to go farther.

Herndon's employees were as cautious as Ryan's; they, too, didn't like being alone at night. And though some had reported seeing shadows out of the corners of their eyes, they all agreed that the spirits probably meant no harm.

Address:	Café Espress 16 N. San Francisco Flagstaff, AZ 86001
Phone:	(928) 774-0541
Hours:	7 a.m.-5 p.m., Sunday-Thursday 7 a.m.-9 p.m., Friday-Saturday

Directions: From Phoenix: Take I-17 North, as it enters Flagstaff it becomes Milton Road, and then turns into Route 66. Continue to San Francisco Street and turn left. Café Espress is on the right.

FLAGSTAFF

CRYSTAL MAGIC

CELLAR DWELLERS

Are there ghosts in the basement?

According to one psychic, a motley crew of ghosts uses the basement at Crystal Magic as their home base, coming and going as they please.

Considering the history of Flagstaff's second oldest building site, it's surprising that the ghosts only number three. Of course, the staff is only aware of three different spirits; perhaps there are others who have yet to come out of the woodwork.

On the site where Crystal Magic (a gift store) now stands, James Vail erected a two-story saloon in 1884, but a Valentine's Day fire destroyed it two years later. Vail rebuilt another tavern in 1887 at the same location, but that one was razed by another major fire in 1888. Liking the location and very determined, Vail constructed a brick building (complete with ghosts) that is still standing.

From 1884 until 1979 the building was used as a saloon except during the period of prohibition when it became a pool hall. In the earliest days it was one of Flagstaff's busiest and rowdiest taverns. Gunfights, stabbings, violence and at least two or three murders all added to the violent reputation of the building.

A former proprietor who shared the basement with Crystal Magic was told that a young girl was murdered in the basement. When decorative balconies were removed in 1915, they were found riddled with bullet holes.

Jill, an employee at Crystal Magic, describes her own encounter with a ghost: "(The ghost) has wavy brown hair, just past her shoulder, and she always has on a white dress. She seems frightened and not at all sure of me."

A psychic, confirming this account, also picked up during a visit once, that there was "a lady in the basement, wearing white." Could Jill's sighting be the ghost of the young girl who was so brutally murdered in the basement?

"A rugged, dirty, old miner comes around quite a bit," Jill continues. "Although he hasn't done anything, I don't feel comfortable with him around. When I'm in the basement getting the vacuum, he gives me the creeps. I can feel him leering at me. When I climb up the stairs, he is usually waiting at the top. Every so often, he ventures upstairs where I've seen him by the candles."

Jill is also aware of another male ghost who lingers upstairs in the book loft. She says she senses his masculine energy; he feels much like the miner but more violent.

Crystal Magic manager Michael Burbank agrees: There are spirits residing in his store. "I haven't seen a ghost yet," he says disappointedly, "but I can certainly feel their presence, more with the miner than with the woman. And I have experienced periphery movement out of the corner of my eye."

The next time you visit Crystal Magic maybe you'll have better luck than Burbank and happen upon one of the ghosts that come and go at this former saloon.

Address:	Crystal Magic 5 N. San Francisco Flagstaff, AZ 86001
Phone:	(928) 779-2528
Hours:	9 a.m.-8 p.m., daily

Directions: From Phoenix: Take I-17 North, as it enters Flagstaff it becomes Milton Road, and then turns into Route 66. Continue to San Francisco Street and turn left. Crystal Magic is on the left.

FLAGSTAFF

HOTEL WEATHERFORD

HEARTBREAK HOTEL?

Presidents, publishers, lawmen and novelists have visited the Weatherford.

So much change has taken place at this late-19th-century hotel, it's surprising there isn't a flock of ghosts refusing to check out. Owner Henry Taylor is just as happy to have it stay that way.

While the hotel basement has its own sense of foreboding, possibly the only actual sighting of a ghost involved a honeymoon couple in a suite on the third floor.

The Hotel Weatherford opened on New Year's Day in 1900. The three-story, 42-room building was considered Flagstaff's finest hotel. Famous guests included President Teddy Roosevelt, publisher William Randolph Hearst and infamous lawman Wyatt Earp. Western novelist Zane Grey wrote *The Call of the Canyon* here while staying as a guest.

In the early 1930s, the hotel started declining and the building went through several transformations. Before operating as a hotel again, it was a billiards hall, a tavern and a theater.

Henry Taylor purchased the building in 1975. Taylor and his wife, Pamela, brought the hotel back to its former glory, but as with any structure more than 100 years old, it's an ongoing process—just like the ghosts who have "haunted" the place forever.

One sighting occurred in Room 55, some time in the 1990s. An employee had been staying in the room for a week, and one morning she awoke to find the ghosts of a bride and groom sitting on her bed. There was speculation that they had been murdered in the room.

Recently, on a quiet Sunday morning, a guest spotted a female ghost in the Zane Grey Ballroom.

Another area of the hotel also causes concern: "I always feel uncomfortable in the basement area," Taylor admits. "I can feel a wall of cold air when I'm down there. The northside basement floor is cement and the southside dirt. This is where I feel the most uneasy."

Taylor and his wife aren't the only ones who are uncomfortable in this section of the basement. Dogs, which seem unusually attuned to supernatural activity, will sometimes refuse to enter the area even after much coaxing from their owners. This happened once to Pamela. Her dog, Mona, started howling and would not cross the dirt floor to reach her owner.

Room 55 is now a storage room, but there are plenty of other rooms you can reserve, especially if you're on your honeymoon. Just don't expect to stay alone together very long: There is at least one other bridal couple here who may have something to say about it.

Address: Hotel Weatherford
23 North Leroux
Flagstaff, AZ 86001

Phone: (928) 779-1919

Directions: From Phoenix: Take I-17 North, as it enters Flagstaff it becomes Milton Road, then turns into Route 66. Continue to North Leroux Street; turn left. Go one block. The Weatherford is on your left.

FLORENCE

TAYLOR'S
BED & BREAKFAST

WHO'S BEEN SLEEPING IN MY BED?

Could a man's devotion to his home continue even after death? The residents of this bed and breakfast think so.

Jesus Martinez began construction on this U-shaped adobe dwelling in 1872, finishing it eight years later. At one point the building was divided into three units containing a store, a meat market and a residence. It was even used as a private hospital in 1882. In 1915, it was converted to a single-family home.

Although the building is more than 100 years old, its ghost is from the recent past. While renovating his newly purchased property into a bed and breakfast in 1981, Eddie Taylor came across opium bottles,

Why does Skeeter keep returning?

needles and syringes. The medical paraphernalia dated back to the property's hospital days, when terminally ill patients from Tucson would travel to Florence to spend their final days here.

Shortly after his discovery of the medical items, Taylor's sleep was interrupted one night by the appearance of an old school chum, "Skeeter," a stocky white-haired man whom Taylor had known since childhood. Skeeter, who had owned the property before Taylor, was, apparently, confused about why his friend was sleeping in what used to be his bedroom.

"What are you doing in my house, Eddie?" Skeeter asked.

"This is my house now. I bought it from Ethel, your wife," Taylor replied. That apparently satisfied Skeeter, because he just laughed and then vanished before Taylor's eyes.

Another time, Taylor's mother, Eve, was visited by Skeeter when she spent the night in the old bedroom. She, too, tried to convince the ghost that the house now belonged to her son, and he was taking very good care of it.

Later, a friend of Taylor's wondered if he, too, would be approached by his friend's ghost if he slept in the room. Sure enough, one night he heard the front door open, after it had been locked, and he felt a presence enter. It was Skeeter, all right, who gruffly asked what this man was now doing in his house.

"I'm Eddie's friend, and it's his house now," the friend explained. "I'm visiting him and wanted to sleep in your old bedroom so I could speak with you."

After a time, Skeeter's wife passed away, and visits to his old bedroom dwindled. His spirit, however, still comes around from time to time. "You can hear him prowling about," Taylor says today, "especially in the kitchen, when he's opening and shutting the metal cupboards. You can also feel cold air as he passes into the kitchen area."

When you make your own reservations, be sure to request the Victorian Room. Skeeter might just show up wondering why you're sleeping in his old bed.

Address:	Taylor's Bed and Breakfast
	321 N. Bailey
	Florence, AZ 85232
Phone:	(520) 868-3497
Email:	cowboyet@earthlink.net

Directions: From Phoenix: Take I-10 East to US60. Take SR79 to Florence. From SR79, exit onto Main Street. Taylor's Bed and Breakfast is on the southeast corner of Bailey and 8th streets.

GLOBE

COBRE VALLEY CENTER FOR THE ARTS

THEATER OF THE CONDEMNED

In 1887, a two-story courthouse and jail were built where the Cobre Valley Center for the Arts now stands. From the start, it was too small for the growing population of the area, but it wasn't until 1906 that the county could come up with the necessary funds needed for a new building. Two years later, the new jail was found to be inadequate, too, so in 1909, a new sheriff's office and jail were built directly east of the courthouse. A catwalk was installed between the two buildings and used primarily for the transfer of prisoners from their jail cells to the courthouse.

One of the ghosts in this historic building is highly territorial and not at all happy with the comings and goings of the various visitors, artists and employees of the Cobre Valley Center. A medium once told employees that the ghost must have been a clerk in his former

life because he tries to keep the fourth floor all to himself. This upper level was used as judge's chambers and law library, which is where, the medium said, the devoted clerk probably spent his working hours.

Former Center employee Tiffany, knows first hand just how possessive this ghost is of his living quarters. The minute she stepped foot on the fourth floor early one morning, he chased her down the stairs. "He didn't chase me physically. It was by his overwhelming presence," she said. "It felt like someone very unlikable wanted me to leave, and I could feel him looking over my shoulder as I ran off."

Although the spirit doesn't welcome humans on "his" floor, he must not mind sharing it with a fellow ghost. The medium learned that in July of 1911, a man, accused of raping and killing two young girls was being held in the county jail which stands directly behind the courthouse. One evening, while the accused was in his cell, an unknown gunman hid himself in the courthouse until after closing. Aiming through a window of the courthouse and across the narrow alleyway, he shot the accused man as he lay in his cell, killing him on the spot.

The medium learned more: the accused man conveyed to her that although he died in his cell, he feels more at home on the fourth floor of the old courthouse. He also revealed that he was sorry for committing such heinous crimes and that he felt that he had been justly punished.

The medium learned that the vengeful gunman is on the premises as well. Employees say it's easy to know when he's around—he's got a cigar in his mouth at all times, they say, and the aroma fills the room when he's "smoking." He has been "seen" wearing 1920s-style clothing and a cowboy hat, and on more than one occasion has been mistaken for a visitor and asked to extinguish his cigar. Very quickly, then, he vanishes into thin air.

Another tale tells the story of Frank Balaam, a local artist originally from England, who volunteered to create a mural in the old courtroom (now used as the Center's theater).

Balaam had just started to paint the framework, not knowing where it would go from there, when he received a phone call from his close friend, Ann. She had been ill, she told him, and was close to death. She was calling, she said, because her doctor had advised her to make her final goodbyes. Balaam asked Ann if he could paint her and her 7-year-old son into his mural to help keep her image alive.

Balaam worked on a small portrait of Ann and her son, Ben. He later added, in the foreground, portraits of his sister, Angela; his mother and father; and his two brothers.

"After Ann's death," Balaam says, "I became aware of a stirring of energy in the darkened theater behind me as I worked, alone with my mural and illuminated by only a single spotlight. I began to sense the century of law and order surrounding me in the still air, and it was as if there was a gathering of entities, a curious audience assembled just out of sight. At this point I realized that this piece of work, which was originally conceived as a simple decorative piece to fill a blank space, had evolved into a project destined to severely challenge my skills in order to create something of great meaning to me.

Balaam's mural in the Cobre Valley Center for the Arts.

"On occasion the air around me grew too intense to work, and more than once I beat a hasty retreat from the imaginary presence of rustlers and outlaws whose last view in life may also have been those same stern walls of the old courtroom. Ghosts from my own past, especially my father," Balaam adds, "came to help, and, between us, we managed to create an unusual world beyond the wall."

The fourth floor isn't the only area that seems to be haunted. Sometime in 1997, a visitor was browsing on the first floor when she felt someone blowing on her neck. When she turned around, however, she discovered no one was there. For 22 years, the old 16-cell jail had occupied this floor, so maybe the "someone" she felt was a former prisoner trying to get her attention.

The third floor is now home to the Copper Cities Community Players, and the old courtroom has been converted into the troupe's theater. But they aren't the only ones to stage dramatic performances here. A certain territorial ghost on the fourth floor is known to put on quite a melodrama, too, now and then, especially if you invade his space.

Address:	Cobre Valley Center for the Arts 101 N. Broad Street Globe, AZ 85501
Phone:	(928) 425-0884
Hours:	10 a.m.-5 p.m., Wednesday-Saturday Noon-5 p.m., Sunday Closed Monday & Tuesday

Directions: From Phoenix: Take I-10 East to US60 exit. Travel east on US60 to Globe. US60 turns left into Broad Street. The Cobre Valley Center is on your left.

GLOBE

OLD GILA COUNTY JAIL

DEAD WOMAN WALKING

Is it Ginney sobbing for her husband—even though she murdered him?

In 1909 a new three-story structure was built to house the criminals of the mining town of Globe and its surrounding areas. It was adjacent to the courthouse by use of a catwalk, which was originally built to transfer prisoners from one building to the other. The ground floor consisted of administrative offices for the Gila County sheriff, and a steel cellblock was located in the rear. The second floor held small cells for women and juveniles and a steel cell block identical to that on the first floor. The third floor consisted of an open trustee dormitory.

"Visitors who are more attuned to the various spirit activity throughout the facility, never stay long," says tour guide Connie Teague of the Historic Globe Main Street Program.

"It can get extremely creepy in here when you're by yourself," she adds. "Several times while I have been at my desk, I could feel a cold spot on my left shoulder, but, I always acknowledge the various ghosts, greeting them in the morning and saying goodnight to them when I close up at night."

Once, out of the corner of her eye, Teague says she caught a glimpse of what appeared to be a man peering through a glass panel that separates the offices from the jail portion of the building. Though she can't explain why, Teague says she thinks what she saw was the ghost of a former employee, not a prisoner.

Some ghosts crave attention and will do anything to get it. Even if it means toying with concrete beds. The bunks in the jailhouse were designed with a metal latch that secures them to the walls. To lower them, one must physically lift the latch. Recently, while on a tour of the women's cell area, one visitor was startled when, as she was leaving the cell area, she heard a loud bang. She was further startled when she saw that one of the bunks—which had been securely in place when she saw it the first time—was now in the reclining position.

"We have a female ghost we call Ginney who is extremely distraught," Teague reports. Often, she adds, this ghost can be heard sobbing. "Although research hasn't been done on her," Teague says, the legend is "that she was in an abusive marriage and had to murder her husband. She was probably protecting herself from her spouse so she shouldn't have been imprisoned in the first place."

When you're exploring the old mining town of Globe, call ahead to arrange for a tour of the Old Gila County Jail. Make sure as you trek through the empty, eerie corridors, however, not to stray too far from Connie Teague. You just never know what restless spirits might be walking right beside you.

Address:	Old Gila County Jail 149 E. Oak Street Globe, AZ 85501
Phone:	(928) 425-9340
Hours:	9 a.m.-12 p.m. Monday through Friday. Call for an appointment for the tour.
Directions:	From Phoenix: Take I-10 East to US60. Travel east to Globe. US60 turns left into Broad. Make a left on Oak and go one block. The Old Gila County Jail is on your left.

GLOBE

JOHNNY'S COUNTRY CORNER

A LONESOME COWBOY?

The building was erected in 1920 and started out as one of Globe's first grocery and mercantile stores. It then housed a car dealership in the 1930s, followed by a Coca-Cola distributing plant; then it became Johnny's Country Corner in 1986.

Painted fire-engine red with white accents, the store, which was built in the shape of the state of Arizona, has something for everyone. One section overflows with antiques and collectibles. Another area displays bolts of fabric and quilting supplies as well as cast iron cookware, enamelware pots, pans and cups. Toward the back of the store, an entire area is devoted to saddlery goods.

It's an interesting place for a ghost to call home.

Some employees are leery about being alone in the building, but Mark Barela has no choice—he is the one who opens up first thing in the morning. "Quite a few times when I first walk into Johnny's, I can feel someone is watching me," Barela says. "Not only is it a creepy feeling, but the hair on my head and arms stands straight up."

Barela, who has been at Johnny's since 1998, also locks up in the evening, so he knows where everything goes. On several occasions, he has not only found items rearranged, but, at times, merchandise has been knocked off the shelves

Does a cowboy haunt Johnny's?

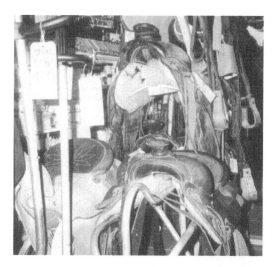

Is the ghost trying them out for size?

and onto the floor. Whatever "spirit" is hanging around has even had the audacity to open up various packages.

As head of the saddlery-goods department, Barela is amazed at what lengths "his" ghost will go to draw attention. "I have arrived in the morning to find the three saddles we have on display have been turned sideways in the aisle. And the security alarm that is on a motion sensor goes off on a regular basis for no apparent reason. Nothing has ever been found that could possibly trigger it to go off."

For whatever reason, the spirit seems attached to Barela and doesn't move too far out of his area. Perhaps he's an old cowhand who still likes hopping on a saddle, or three saddles in this case.

Address:	Johnny's Country Corner 383 S. Hill Street Globe, AZ 85501
Phone:	(928) 425-8208
Hours:	9 a.m.-5:30 p.m., Tuesday-Saturday

Directions: From Phoenix: Take I-10 East to US60. Travel east to Globe. Upon reaching Globe, follow the truck route to the stop light at Hill Street. Turn left and go 1 block—Johnny's is on the right.

GREER

WHITE MOUNTAIN LODGE

A REAL 'WHODUNIT'

Is it Mary or Agnes that visits the White Mountain Lodge?

Mary and Charlie Bast, owners of the White Mountain Lodge, like to host Mystery Weekends, incorporating their guests as the characters. By the end of each weekend, the "whodunit" is solved, and guests go home knowing who committed the "murder."

There have been times, though, when guests checked out without ever fully understanding what *really* happened to them. Like the time, for instance, when a 16-year-old boy, who, in the middle of the night, came downstairs to get some hot chocolate. Before satisfying his sweet tooth, he got an eyeful when he noticed the rocking chair in the living room rocking back and forth on its own.

A young couple in Room 2 may still be questioning each other on the female ghost they saw in the middle of the night one time recently. The apparition, wearing a long flowing gown, was seen in the back yard of the White Mountain Lodge at 2 a.m. The Basts were called, but Mary couldn't help because she was as mystified as her lodgers.

"The White Mountain Lodge was built in 1892 when Marion and Agnes Lund resided here," says Mary. "They raised eight children, from 1904 until 1940. Maybe Agnes is the one we saw in the back yard that time. One of our other guests who stayed in Room 6 also felt a strong female presence once. A 'very comforting feeling' is how she described it."

Mary received an e-mail once from a couple staying in Room 5. They had checked out a day earlier. "The husband woke up in the middle of the night and was shocked to find a man and a woman, dressed in old-fashioned clothing, sitting in the chairs in their room." The guests

The chairs in Room 5.

told Mary that their ghostly late-night visitors looked like the couple whose portrait was hanging in the second-floor hallway. "He felt that they were trying to communicate with him, but he couldn't comprehend just what they were trying to tell him. The next evening as they were getting ready to turn in, the man started to get scared that they would have a repeat performance so they left immediately."

The photograph, which dates back to 1880, is of very distant relatives of Charlie Bast. The irony, however, is that none of Charlie's family ventured out West to Greer, so it's a mystery why they made a surprise visit to Room 5 and why they didn't stay long enough to spend some time with their relatives, Charlie and Mary.

If you spend a Mystery Weekend at the White Mountain Lodge, hopefully you'll leave with no question unanswered.

Address:	White Mountain Lodge
	140 Main
	Greer, AZ 85927

Phone: (928) 735-7568

Directions: From Phoenix: Take I-10 East to US60. Travel east to Globe. Take SR260 southeast to exit 373 to Greer.

HOOVER DAM

A FEW 'DAMMED' SOULS

Winged Statues at Hoover Dam commemorate those who worked and died during the building process.

Quite a few people mistakenly think that Hoover Dam is located wholly in Nevada. But part of it lies in Arizona. Which side is haunted? Arizona or Nevada? Or both?

First, some background:

To harness the Colorado River and to fill Southern California's water and electricity supply, Congress passed the Boulder Canyon Project Act in 1928, authorizing the Hoover Dam to be built.

Construction Superintendent Frank T. Crowe was determined to make a name for himself building the largest dam in the world in the shortest time, even if it meant he had to drive his workers to death – which, sadly, he did. Construction on this massive project began in 1931 and took less than five years to complete. To make sure he reached that goal, Crowe had some 5,000 men working round the clock.

Today, visitors often inquire about the legend surrounding the dam's construction—that ghosts of the workers entombed in the concrete haunt the area. Tour guides chuckle and tell them that it would have been impossible for anyone to be buried in the concrete. The dam was constructed of interlocking blocks, built one on top of the other. Each block was only five feet high, but each pour was only ankle deep. So, if a worker had fallen into a block, he would have been able to climb out on his own.

Even so, 96 industrial fatalities occurred—from drowning, rockslides, falls from the high canyon walls, truck accidents and heavy-equipment mishaps. Many others met their demise through illness, of course, via heart attacks, natural causes or other medical conditions associated with their work on the dam. During the summer of 1933, heat prostration killed one worker every two days.

Though the professional guides avoid sharing information about the ghosts who haunt the dam, when pressed, one or two employees will 'fess up. According to them and a handful of visitors, two spirits call Hoover Dam their home.

"An apparition of a construction worker has been seen in one of the dam's two power houses," says dam historian Dennis McBride. Reportedly, "He is always dressed in overalls and tries to communicate with you. Although his mouth is forming words, no sound comes out."

Who is this ghost? Records were kept on all of the unfortunate deaths at the dam, but because there weren't any photos to match up with the names, the identity of this young apparition remains a mystery. Overalls were the usual attire when the dam was being built so most likely he was a construction worker.

The second ghost has been seen at the Nevada valve house. "We think he's also a construction worker but from a more recent time," McBride says. "In 1980 a worker was on the mezzanine floor and when he leaned against the rail, it gave out. He was killed instantly when he landed on his head two stories down. This spirit can be seen entering one of the elevators. When visitors or employees are waiting for an elevator, he likes to startle them by being in the elevator when the door opens."

A group of psychics toured the dam in 1997, but the only ghosts that have actually been seen were the two mentioned above. Many "presences" were felt, however, specifically on the powerhouse roof. One psychic had the feeling that the dam was surrounded by guardian spirits of the men who worked there. She claimed they were in guardianship over the project that was such an important part of the workers' lives. While wandering the rooftop, the psychic stopped cold when she said she felt a great deal of anger and obstinacy from a spirit who fought passing over despite help from the dam's guardians.

Another psychic felt the presence of a spirit who smelled of booze and followed the psychic around. A suicide from the dam's later years had involved an alcoholic whose corpse, when officials found it, reeked of liquor. Could it have been this alcoholic's ghost trailing behind the psychics?

McBride says he knows of a third ghost who lives in a much more comfortable environment. "I work in the Boulder City/Hoover Dam Museum, which is located at the Boulder Dam Hotel. While I was working in my office one day, I felt something very heavy behind me. I turned and there was a ghost wearing a white shirt. I've only seen him once, although I do feel his presence from time to time. I work by myself so it is nice to have some company every so often, even if it is a ghost."

Unsubstantiated tales of ghosts swimming in the water and even the ghost of a night watchman who patrols the area late at night have also been reported.

With all the tragic deaths that occurred at Hoover Dam, there may be quite a few ghosts who have yet to make their presence known, so beware. If you don't get a concrete sighting of one on the tour, the passing "presence" of another dammed soul may still await you.

Address:	Hoover Dam US93—Arizona/Nevada border
Phone:	(702) 293-3517
Hours:	After the events of Sept. 11, 2001, guided tours of the dam were suspended. The visitor center is opened for limited operation. The theater, exhibits and overlook are opened to the public. Call ahead for updated information.

Directions: From Phoenix: Take US 60/89 northwest (it is known as Grand Avenue) to Wickenburg. Take US93 to Kingman (it joins up with I-40 before you reach Kingman.) Continue northwest on US93 to Hoover Dam.

HUMBOLDT

RIATA PASS GALLERY

A PAUSE FOR REFLECTION

Check out the mirror images!

It may be an auction house and antique store now, but Riata Pass Gallery was originally Humboldt's first saloon. The saloon opened in the late 19th-century and was purchased in the early 1900s by Mr. & Mrs. Shelby. Although the couple is long deceased, the Shelbys were thought to have been on the premises in the 1950s when their old saloon became the Riata Pass Steakhouse.

A fascinating pair, the Shelbys had a daily routine of brewing coffee between 4 and 5 p.m. Whenever the afternoon aroma started drifting through the building, employees knew without checking their watches, that it was 4 o'clock.

What wasn't so pleasant, however, was Mr. Shelby's other "daily routine"—pinching his waitresses on their bottoms. During its steak-house days, the servers claimed that old Mr. Shelby kept up this routine—even as a ghost. They all had the same complaint: a pinch would be felt, but no one was ever around to blame.

Once, while cleaning up on the upper level of the restaurant, a waitress glanced down and in a mirror she saw couples dancing to the rhythm of music. She thought that all the customers had gone for the night, so she went downstairs to tell the couples that the steakhouse was closed. She soon realized, however, that she was the only person in the building. Back upstairs, she couldn't resist looking one more time and she saw, once again, images of people dancing in the same mirror.

Riata Pass Gallery was established in 1999 when Bob Greene purchased the building. The gallery's pieces fit right in with the town's historic surroundings. Old firearms, battlefield memorabilia, antiques, and Indian and Western artifacts are just some of the items that go up for bid.

From the start, Greene had been aware that Humboldt's first saloon was occupied by ghosts. Who they were, he wasn't sure, but he accepted the fact and dug in at his new shop, planning renovations to keep the building as close to its original character as possible. One day, while installing new plumbing, the water lines were disconnected as a matter of routine. The spirits had a different idea, however, and kept the water on. After much wrangling, one of the workers who'd been aware of the building's ghostly lore, finally told them to stop playing with the water flow, and that did the trick. The water stayed off.

Greene has had to talk with the ghosts as well. A couple of weeks after installing an alarm system, Greene heard it go off two or three times a night. "I told them I didn't mind the pranks, and they could have fun, but I warned them to stop playing with the alarms and not to break anything expensive," Greene says. "They must have been paying attention because things seemed to calm down quite a bit."

The ghosts still like to shut the water off when someone is showering and tinker with the lights, causing them to go on and off. Footsteps as well as muffled conversations can also be occasionally heard.

The spirits do come in handy from time to time, says Greene. Once, "while I was trying to coax my dog out of an office, something grabbed me on my shoulders, spun me around and in that exact minute, an expensive painting fell off the wall, landing right into my hands," he says. "Since I was alone, the credit has to be given to one of the ghosts."

About the occurrences, Greene once consulted a Native American spiritualist who came into the gallery one day. "He suggested that if we had an evil spirit, he could do a cleansing and blessing, which would clear the building of the ghosts, but I declined," Greene says. "I'm happy with them. They're welcome to stay as long as they want."

Come in and browse or attend an auction but the Victorian mirror that had images of dancing couples isn't for sale. And, neither are the ghosts. Bob's hanging on to them!

Address:	Riata Pass Gallery
	3525 S. Hwy. 69
	Humboldt, AZ 86329
Phone:	(928) 632-8000
Hours:	Call for hours.

Directions: From Phoenix: Take I-17 North, exit at 262, making a left onto SR69. In approximately twenty miles, the gallery will be on your right-hand side.

JEROME

CONNOR HOTEL

RE-LIVING IN THE LAP OF LUXURY

When the Connor Hotel opened its doors in 1898, it was considered one of the West's most upscale lodging establishments. Each of its 23 rooms was furnished with call bells, electricity and individual wood stoves. One paid for those luxuries, however; a dollar a night was extravagant in those days.

Within two years, the hotel burnt to the ground twice, but Dave Connor, the owner, was one of the few in Jerome who carried fire insurance and was able to rebuild both times. After it reopened in August of 1899, it once again earned the reputation of being a first-class hotel.

Maybe the ghosts who refuse to check out are on to something. If you're going to haunt a building, it might as well be a first-class joint, right?

What? No spirits in the Spirit Room?

After years of renovations by today's owners, David and Sandy Conlin, and their daughter, Anne, the Connor Hotel has once again been restored to its original opulence.

The spirits who invade the hotel keep themselves well hidden. Although apparitions haven't been seen—yet—there's no doubt in Anne's mind that they're there.

"In 1999 a satellite television installer from Phoenix was having difficulty setting up the equipment," Ann says, "so I suggested that he spend the night instead of driving back to the Valley only to return the following day. He stayed in Room 1, but at about 2 a.m. he left and spent the remainder of the night in his van. After hearing another person mention that the hotel was haunted, he finally admitted why he bolted to his car so abruptly in the middle of the night. Turns out, he heard unusual noises, scratching sounds and women whispering. If that wasn't eerie enough, he said he felt a cold presence covering his body.

"Room 5," Anne continues, "is haunted as well. Again, no one has ever seen anything, but electrical malfunctions are constant. Guests who have palm-pilot organizers always complain that the clocks and calendars don't work. The television set is always blinking on and off.

Who plays with the electrical appliances in Room 5?

And the alarm clock will suddenly go off even though there might not have been any guests in the room for a week."

Anne's cousin, Tisa, says she will always remember what happened to her in a restroom on the second floor. While she was in the facility, she heard her name called out. She felt uneasy, but when there wasn't an answer to her question, "Who's there?" she thought it was just her imagination playing tricks on her. A few minutes later she heard her name called out again. It was a man's voice although very soft and distinct. Tisa left rather quickly, but didn't run into anyone on her way down the stairs. She had been alone on the second floor.

Professional spirit photographers Sharon Gill and Dave Oester paid a visit once to the Connor Hotel and were rewarded by their efforts. They claim to have captured on film the energy vortex of an invisible entity on the stairway. Although they say they felt like something was following them upstairs, it wasn't visible to them until their film was developed.

The Connor Hotel's tavern, the Spirit Room Bar, is not named for the spirits that haunt the hotel. In fact, when asked what kind of ghostly activity occurs in the historic bar, the answer is always "None."

Your best bet to experience a touch of the supernatural would be to reserve a room on the second floor. And if things get too "scratchy" in Room 1, remember the repairman's fix: You can always go outside and sleep in your van.

Address: Connor Hotel
                  164 Main St.
                  Jerome, AZ 86331

Phone: (928) 634-5006

Directions: From Phoenix: Take I-17 North to SR260. Go northwest to Cottonwood and turn onto SR 89A. Take SR89A into Jerome where it turns into Hull. Stay on Hull to Main Street.

JEROME

THE HAUNTED HAMBURGER

IF I HAD A HAMMER...

Ghosts dangle from the ceiling at the Haunted Hamburger, suggesting that the owner may be delinquent in taking down last year's Halloween decorations. But maybe the owners, Eric and Michelle Jurisin, are just paying homage to their ghost. Unfortunately or fortunately, depending how you look at it, their lone ghost has gone into hiding. At least for now.

A harbinger of things to come?

When Eric purchased the old building on Clark Street, it had been vacant for six years. Not much is known about the history of it except it had been the Wykoff Apartments in 1920. When he started refurbishing, it didn't take Eric long to realize that hammers had a way of disappearing in his newly purchased structure.

"When the first and second hammer disappeared I just thought I was getting absent-minded," Jurisin says. "I bought a third hammer, at a cost of $30, and after that vanished, I decided to use a rock. It was getting too expensive to replace all of them! Once, while I was having lunch at a small deli, the proprietor asked me if I had seen the ghost yet. Bill Watkins, the previous owner of my building, used to complain to him that a ghost kept hiding his hammer. I felt better knowing I wasn't just forgetting where I left my tools. Now, I could put the blame on a ghost."

When he returned from lunch, Jurisin discovered that all three of his hammers were out in the open. One was on top of the washing machine; another on the counter top; and the third hammer was lying on top of a dresser.

A repairman was also once a mark for the Haunted Hamburger's ghost. A wrench, which he had with him at all times while he was on the ladder, simply vanished into thin air, turning up later that day in the kitchen.

"I would arrive some mornings to find hot water coming out full blast from the faucets," Eric says. "Other times it would be slamming doors or the lights suddenly would go on. Since the restaurant opened though, it seems as if the mischief has ceased."

Has the Haunted Hamburger's spirit moved to different quarters or will he make another appearance at the Jurisins' restaurant when the mood strikes?

Is the ghost in hiding?

One thing's for sure: If Eric's hammer turns up missing again, he'll no doubt find another big rock.

Address: The Haunted Hamburger
410 N. Clark Street
Jerome, AZ 86331

Phone: (928) 634-0554

Hours: 11 a.m.-9 p.m., daily

Directions: From Phoenix: Take I-17 North to SR260. Go northwest to Cottonwood and turn onto SR89A. Take SR89A into Jerome where it turns into Hull. Stay on Hull to Main Street. On Main make a right; Main becomes Clark Street. Haunted Hamburger is on the left.

KINGMAN

HOTEL BRUNSWICK

THREE GHOSTS FIND ROOMS

A historic building with a spirited past!

Not much is known about the ghosts in this 1909 hotel: A gentleman, a young girl and a third ghost in Room 202. The gender of No. 3 is unknown, but the staff believes it is probably a female because the spirit is meticulous about the position of a footstool.

Messrs. Thompson & Mulligan formed a partnership to build the Hotel Brunswick, the first three-story building in the surrounding area of Kingman. The hotel earned an upscale reputation by using Waterford crystal, brass beds and a telephone in every room. It's no wonder that railroad passengers and out-of-town guests loved staying at this chic establishment.

The partnership soured, however, in only three years. To solve the rift equally, the men put up a dividing wall to create two separate hotels. Thompson ended up with 25 rooms and the restaurant, and Mulligan 25 rooms and the bar.

Eventually, Joe Otero, who had previously purchased the Thompson side, was finally able to obtain Mulligan's half as well. He removed the wall, turning it back into one hotel.

For more than 20 years, the once elegant hotel stood vacant. When they reopened the property in February 1999, new owners Gerald and Jessie Guedon realized that they not only acquired a dream hotel, they got one that came complete with its own ghosts.

The spirit of an old gentleman had been seen in Room 212, so Jessie was happy when one of her guests decided to do some detective work on past deaths that might have occurred there.

Room 212. Wealthy W. D. McCright died in this room. Does he return to visit with the guests?

"On September 7, 2000, Tina Dupuy, a young screenwriter and researcher from Los Angeles found herself stranded in Kingman due to car trouble," Jessie says. Staying at the Hotel Brunswick, Dupuy became intrigued with the ghost stories and decided to do some research at the local museum. Pulling out the old microfiche files, she came across an article from the *Kingman Daily Miner*, dated March 13, 1915, covering the death of wealthy, 73-year-old W.D. McCright who died in his room:

> *"W.D. McCright was found dead in his room at the Brunswick Hotel last Sunday morning, death coming without warning. He had evidently arisen at the usual hour and was making his morning absolutions when the grim terror called. Not making his appearance at the usual hour, Mr. Miller went to his room and found him lying on the floor, dead, with a towel in his hands."*

Not only did the previous owners keep this room off-limits because they felt it was haunted, but, according to one of their employees, they refused to even talk about Room 212. The Guedons, however, have always rented it out, and so far, no guests have left in the middle of the night. Spirits have visited some of their guests, Jessie says, usually around 2:00 in the morning.

Complete with a balcony overlooking Route 66, Room 202 has a spirit that likes to move things around. An employee once found the mattress had been shoved to a different area of the room when she returned with some fresh linens, even though the door had been locked. And housekeeping repeatedly finds a small footstool moved from one spot to another.

A little-girl ghost is said to wander about on the second and third floors, leaving behind a trail of pennies.

The Guedons love hearing about unexplained occurrences in their hotel, so feel free to let your imagination go here, especially if you reserve Rooms 202 or 212.

Address: Hotel Brunswick
                 315 E. Andy Devine
                 Kingman, AZ 86401

Phone: (928) 718-1800

Directions: From Phoenix: Take US 89/60 (Grand Avenue) to Wickenburg. Turn onto US 93 and follow it to Kingman via I-40. Take Exit 48, following Route 66 signs into downtown Kingman. The Hotel Brunswick is on your left, approximately one mile.

MESA

THE LANDMARK RESTAURANT

PARANORMAL SEEMS TO BE THE NORM HERE!

Don and Candy Ellis opened their new restaurant, TheLandmark, on New Year's Day in 1982. The building is full of history, dating back to 1908 when it began its life as a Mormon Church. The church was originally housed in what is now the main dining room. Downstairs were the Sunday School rooms, and through the years two additional buildings were built for social events. In the late 1930s, a smaller structure was built as a Boy Scout meeting room.

In the 1950s the Mormon Church outgrew the buildings

Who are the ghosts of the Landmark?

and moved to larger quarters. An insurance company was in the building for several years, and in 1963 it became the original campus of Mesa Community College. Nine years later Rouch's Schoolhouse Restaurant served its first meal. When The Landmark took over, ghosts were probably the furthest thing from Candy Ellis' mind.

"I was busy one day, playing hostess and doing a million other things at the same time when this was thrown in my face," Ellis says, laughing. "One of my customers was in town attending a paranormal conference and she came in for dinner. She told me that she immediately felt a presence as soon as she walked into the restaurant. She went on to tell me that the presence was connected to me, adding that there were unsettled souls throughout the entire building. She sat in the main dining room and was just beside herself. She kept emphasizing that there were lots of souls milling about, too many presences, and finally announced that she was too upset and just couldn't eat her dinner. With that," Ellis says, "she left."

Ellis might have been surprised that The Landmark had spirits here and there, but her employees suspected all along that there was at least one ghost in the late-19th-century building. All of the employees have mentioned hearing strange noises and lights that go on and off. Others have said that the downstairs is more haunted than the upstairs. One staff member guessed that the presence she sensed once was that of a very troubled female.

There is an area right in front of the waitress station where employees trip for no apparent reason. There isn't a rug or mat, which would cause anyone to stumble, and the floor isn't uneven. When one of the waitresses loses her footing, their ghost always gets the blame. It's the only explanation they can find for their constant tripping. The spirit is also known to say "psst" very softly in employees' ears.

When you dine at The Landmark take extra time to go downstairs where there is a large display of historic photos, some dating back more than 100 years ago. They line the walls of the hallway as well as the dining rooms. Keep in mind though, that some employees insist that this is the most haunted area of the building.

Address:	The Landmark Restaurant 809 W. Main Street Mesa, AZ 85201
Phone:	(480) 962-4652
Hours:	Lunch: 11 a.m.-3 p.m., Monday through Saturday Dinner: 3 p.m.-9 p.m., Monday through Saturday Dinner: 11 a.m.-7 p.m., Sundays

Directions: From Phoenix: Take SR202 East, exit onto Alma School Road. Go south on Alma School to Main. Left on Main to next light. The Landmark restaurant is on the southwest corner of Extension and Main.

PHOENIX

AUNT CHILADA'S
AT SQUAW PEAK

AT THIS BAR, THEY <u>DID</u> SERVE MINERS!

At Aunt Chilada's you get the whole enchilada: excellent food, historic ambience and at least one ghost. Unfortunately, the friendly Victorian lady has only been sighted once and that was in 1983.

Aunt Chilada's North Room was built on the foundation of the only general store serving the laborers working the Rico-Mercury Mine. The mining smelters were in full operation throughout the nearby mountain range in what is now The Pointe at Squaw Peak residential area. "When the miners walked the draw to the general store, they would get high from inhaling the mercury wafting from the mines," owner Candice Nagel explains. "By the time they reached the store, they were dreamy, which is how the name of the street 'Dreamy Draw,' came about."

When mining ceased in the 1930s, the century-old building went from being a general store to a restaurant and saloon. The Peek Steakhouse got its name from a uniquely placed and somewhat revealing window set in the ceiling of the bar (now the Tienda). Throughout the night, scantily clad women would climb into the attic and perform a hootchy-kootchy dance while patrons sneaked a peek through the window. This unusual entertainment proved to be popular, and guests from as far away as the Camelback Inn and the Arizona Biltmore Hotel would ride over on horseback, just to enjoy a cool libation and "keep their heads up."

George's Olé, a popular watering hole, occupied the building in the 1960s, and in 1983 it was renamed Aunt Chilada's. Candice and Ken Nagel have owned the restaurant since 1995 and love the colorful history as much as their patrons do.

"The general store had a cellar beneath it where the owner would keep ice in gunnysacks to keep the fruit fresh," Candice says. "One day the husband just disappeared and was never seen again and after that, the cellar entrance disappeared, as if it had never existed!"

Was the lady in white lace waiting for her banquet date?

Candice went on. "The owner's wife was very young with either an Indian or Hispanic background. One of my daughters and Shulamite Alaniz, one of our chefs, are convinced that they sometimes hear her talking to someone. Perhaps her missing husband?"

Shulamite who has been a chef at Aunt Chilada's for more than 20 years, recalls the day when she saw the apparition of a young lady. "It was in 1983, and I saw her as plain as day, sitting in a chair in the banquet room. She was wearing a lace, high-collar white dress that dated back to the late 1800s. She looked to be in her late teens or early 20s and had long blond hair."

Alaniz caught sight of the ghost while renovations were being done. The only other people on the premises were male construction workers and Alaniz's husband.

"I'm clairvoyant and I can feel her when she's around," Alaniz says. "She seems to be waiting for someone, maybe a husband or boyfriend. And for some reason she doesn't come around in the summer or spring; it's just in the fall and winter months. She loves festivals, happy times and dancing.

"She still has the child in her and can be quite mischievous. She turns lights on and off, and we'll find an open door that earlier was locked. You don't experience an eerie feeling in the banquet room where she stays but you can sometimes encounter cold chills."

Other employees swap stories of their various experiences with their resident ghost. Dave, a maintenance man, related the time that a fan turned on, even though it wasn't plugged into a wall socket. Doug, one of the managers, has seen items roll across the floor where the old general store had been.

The young lady that Ms. Alaniz spotted in the banquet room couldn't be the late wife of the original storeowner. She was of Indian or Hispanic origin and certainly wouldn't have had blonde hair. So, are there two female ghosts occupying Aunt Chilada's? And, what about an elderly gentleman that Alaniz says she "feels" from time to time? An old miner? The original store owner? Drop by and see if you can sort them all out—while you're feasting on your own enchilada.

Address: Aunt Chilada's at Squaw Peak
7330 N. Dreamy Draw Drive
Phoenix, AZ 85020

Phone: (602) 944-1286

Hours: 11 a.m.-11 p.m., Sunday-Thursday
11 a.m.-1 a.m., Friday-Saturday

Directions: From Phoenix: Take I-17 to Northern exit. Travel east to 16th St. Make a right on 16th Street. At the first light, which is Morten, make a left and go two blocks into The Pointe Squaw Peak. Aunt Chilada's is on the southwest corner of Morten and Dreamy Draw Drive.

PHOENIX

PIONEER ARIZONA LIVING HISTORY MUSEUM

PHANTOMS OF THE OPERA HOUSE

The Victorian House at Pioneer Arizona Living History Museum

Twenty-eight historical buildings make up this late-19th-century village with an assortment of ghosts in various buildings. Take your pick—the Opera House, the Victorian House, Jack's Farm House and the Pioneer Restaurant and Saloon—they are all haunted.

Even though the restaurant was built as recently as 1967, it is not exempt from a ghost. Kathy, a former proprietor, named him "Slim" when she first saw him saunter through the restaurant. She described him to her coworkers as a slender man who looked like a cowboy, down to his boots.

"It's hard to explain, but I walked right through Slim once," Operations Manager Juanita Buckley says. "I've never felt anything like it before. It was such an eerie feeling. When I told Kathy about it, she just laughed and reinforced my exact feelings; I went through his presence. I've never felt anything like it before or after. I can also feel his presence right behind me as I move about in the restaurant. Maybe he came along with the authentic furniture."

The 100-year-old Victorian House was relocated from Phoenix to Pioneer. One of the previous owners might have decided to come along as well.

A couple, who were visiting along with a group of Civil War re-enactors, had the opportunity to spend the night in the Victorian House. Because all the beds were singles, the husband and wife slept in separate rooms. He slept in the children's bedroom and woke up in the middle of the night to find a woman pulling the covers over him. His visitor was old and had her hair pulled back. He later saw her in a picture hanging on the wall.

The Opera House was moved brick by brick from Prescott where the famous opera singer Lily Langtry sang. Buckley says she can feel the presence of a male and hears footsteps when she is alone. Could the footsteps belong to Slim, who has also been seen in this building? Or is there another ghost roaming about?

Jack's House, an old farmhouse transported from Phoenix, is where the ghost of a little girl resides. One of the workers has seen her on several occasions and couldn't help but notice how sad and upset she always looked. The volunteer thought that perhaps the doll that was on display belonged to the girl. Noticing how the doll wasn't dressed very nicely she decided to make a new outfit for it. She made a little blue dress with an apron over it and a matching blue bonnet resembling what the child's ghost always had on. It must have pleased the spirit because the next time she was seen, she appeared happy.

There are 25 other historic buildings, and if you look hard enough, you might find a ghost that has gone unnoticed by the staff and visitors.

Address:	Pioneer Arizona Living History Museum 3901 W. Pioneer Road Phoenix, AZ 85086
Phone:	(623) 465-1052

Museum Hours: 9 a.m.-5 p.m., Wednesday-Sunday, October 1-June 1 and from 9 am.-3 p.m. June 2-Sept. 30. The Pioneer Restaurant & Saloon is open until 1 a.m.

Directions: From Phoenix: Take I-17 North to Pioneer Road (Exit 225). Follow the signs.

PHOENIX

HOTEL SAN CARLOS

THE PITTER-PATTER OF LITTLE GHOSTLY FEATS

Washington, D.C., has the ghost of Abe Lincoln; Justice, Illinois has claim to Resurrection Mary; San Jose, California, has bragging rights to Sara Winchester; and the ghost of Phoenix, hands-down, is Leone Jensen.

The Hotel San Carlos sits downtown surrounded by a mixture of historic buildings, sleek skyscrapers and BankOne Ballpark. Owner, Greg Melikian, refers to the San Carlos as "the gem of Phoenix" and is determined to preserve its historic charm.

The hotel was built in 1928, but the history of this piece of property actually goes back further than that. The San Carlos sits over a well of sacred water that had been

The historic Hotel San Carlos

used by ancient Native Americans to worship their Gods of Wisdom. In 1874 the first schoolhouse in north-central Phoenix was erected on this site. It started out as a one-room, dirt-floor adobe building and within five years expanded into a two-story brick structure. It operated as a school until it closed in 1916.

Since 1929 three noisy little boys have disturbed guests on all floors of the San Carlos. One guest spotted the children running down the hallway but when he caught up with them, they disappeared before his eyes. Housekeeping staff periodically hear giggles of youngsters coming from the basement, and other employees have heard balls bouncing on the floors throughout the building.

Leone Jensen's last steps?

Leone Jensen took advantage of the seven-floor hotel by hurling herself from the roof on May 7, 1928, just two months after the San Carlos opened its doors. Only 22 at the time, Leone was despondent when the love of her life, a bellboy at a nearby hotel, broke off their relationship. Her white form has been seen floating up the staircase on the seventh floor that leads to the roof. She has also been seen walking down the hallways and, on occasion, leaning over the guests as they sleep.

Bring earplugs with you in case three little boys get rambunctious the night you stay at the Hotel San Carlos. And the best chance to catch a glimpse of Leone is to reserve a room on the seventh floor.

Address: Hotel San Carlos
                202 N. Central
                Phoenix, AZ 85004

Phone: (602) 253-4121

Directions: From Phoenix: Take I-17 to McDowell; exit east onto McDowell. Turn right at Central. Hotel San Carlos is on the northwest corner of Central and Monroe.

TEETER HOUSE

LADY GHOSTS GET TEA'D OFF!

Eliza Teeter's home in Heritage Square.

The Teeter House is an "authentic Victorian Tea Room" complete with its own ghost. Located in Heritage Square, the Midwestern-style bungalow was built in 1899 by Leon Bouvier, who used it as rental property. Eliza Teeter purchased the home in 1911 and used it as a rental as well. Eight years later she moved into the house, remaining there until her death in 1965. Lynne Behringer, present owner of the charming tea room, feels that Eliza is still on the premises.

"Eliza was a tough survivor," Behringer says. "She had five children, and when she used her home as a boarding house she not only cooked for her guests but ironed for them as well. But, she still made time to play the organ at her church."

The first few months after Behringer opened the Teeter House, she says she couldn't help but feel unwelcome. She was constantly losing things (with help from her mischievous spirit), and 80 percent of anything mechanical had to be repaired.

"She must have been testing me, but apparently I passed muster," Behringer says. "I can tell Ms. Teeter is happy with me now; items aren't disappearing as often."

Amanda, hired as a cook, didn't have to wait long before she was introduced to the antics of Eliza. On her first day, she was sitting on a bar stool when she heard her name called. Looking all over, she realized she was alone in the room. When Behringer saw her a few moments later, she knew that Amanda must have seen a ghost. "Her eyes were as big as saucers and she was white as can be," Behringer says. "I explained to Amanda that it was just Eliza's way of welcoming her to the Teeter House."

One afternoon Behringer was with a guest when Eliza happened to be in one of her playful moods. In the parlor they witnessed a miniature corner piece elevate into the air, leap over a teapot and land in the middle of the room.

Another employee, Tia, observed how the former owner always insists on having her own way. In the Garden Room where Teeter passed away, a flower arrangement that had been sitting on a small display next to a table, somehow made it onto the table. Tia watched in amazement as the arrangement scooted to the center. Eliza must favor this room, as this is the only area where staff members have glimpsed her ghostly presence.

Eliza Teeter lived in her house for 54 years, which should entitle any ghost the right to stay as long as she desires!

Address: The Teeter House
                622 E. Adams Street
                Phoenix, AZ 85004

Phone: (602) 252-4682

Hours: 11 a.m.-4 p.m., Tuesday-Saturday
                Noon-4 p.m., Sunday
                6:30 p.m.-11:00 p.m., Friday and Saturday evenings|
                Afternoon Tea by reservation

Directions: From Phoenix: Take I-17 to 7th Street; exit and travel north. Heritage Square is between Adams and Monroe Streets.

VALLEY YOUTH THEATRE

A BRITISH INVASION

Will the Victorian visitors make a return engagement?

There's no doubt in Linda Schneider's mind how the building on Central and Fillmore became home to two very British ladies.

When Del Webb began his contracting career, one of his first projects was to build a car dealership on this site. The paint and body shop stood on one corner, and on another corner was the car dealership.

An Elks or Moose lodge occupied the building next, complete with a one-lane bowling alley and a restaurant for its members. An antique mall followed, but when that closed, the building was vacant until Schneider and her husband moved into the building in 1989.

The Schneiders made the most of the large structure by using the front half for their Improv Theater group. The Adobe Oven Bakery, also owned by the couple, was located in the back half of the structure. An apartment, between the actors group and the bakery, served as the couple's residence. A long hallway led up to the Adobe Oven, and next to the door was a window where customers could peer in.

Each night, the staff would make the next day's pastries so they would be ready for early customers. Once, while preparing his dough, a former employee, Bob, noticed he had an audience.

"Six months after we opened the Adobe Oven Bakery, Bob asked me if I had ever seen the two ladies that had visited him the previous night," Schneider recalls. "They were standing at the window by the door watching him work. At first he thought they might have been friends of mine even though it was very late. But then he realized that he could see right through them. He's not one to be frightened easily, so he just took the two ghosts in stride. Before Bob quit, they stopped by to see him a few more times, always standing by the door. Although he acknowledged them, introducing himself and explaining what he was in the process of making at that particular moment, the women would only smile."

Three weeks later, Schneider looked up and saw that Bob's previous visitors were watching her from the doorway entrance. "One of them asked me in a marvelous, very British accent, where Bob was," Schneider says, sounding very British herself. "I explained to them that he had left for another place of employment. Their reply was, 'Oh, all right.' Even though they came back a few more times, they never spoke again. But they always stood in the entrance, never stepping a foot into the bakery."

Both women, who appeared to be in their late 40s or early 50s, were garbed in Victorian clothing and one carried a small purse. The frilly lace caps they were wearing looked to Schneider to be made of muslin fabric. Their hair was pulled back into severe-looking buns, but they didn't resemble each other, so chances are they weren't sisters.

Schneider speculates: "They were middle-class women, and, by their appearance, I would guess that they were dressed to go out visiting. Maybe they were with some friends for afternoon tea when some kind of disaster struck. There was probably an emotional attachment to where it was that they passed away."

Later, Schneider says she was going to warn them of some major renovations that she and her husband were going to do in the building so they wouldn't be alarmed, but she never saw them again.

Schneider also once agreed to host a "rave" dance party in the building. "I didn't know what to expect with the rave but it sure wasn't *that*!" she says. "If the noise from the construction didn't drive them away, then the party surely must have. We didn't move out of the building until 1994, but I never did see them again, nor any other ghost for that matter."

The building, now home to the Valley Youth Theatre, has changed since the British Victorian ladies dropped in. It has since been gutted, and the exterior walls are probably the only things any of the ghosts would recognize.

Did the prim and proper females from a different era come over with an antique piece of furniture from Great Britain? Were they having afternoon tea and scones in a friend's parlor and in one split second found themselves in the antique mall on First Street and Fillmore? This is Schneider's theory, but she can't help but wonder where her ghosts disappeared to.

Address:	Valley Youth Theatre 525 N. First Street Phoenix, AZ
Phone:	(602) 253-8188
Hours:	Call for production times.

Directions: From Phoenix: Take I-17 to McDowell; exit east onto McDowell. Turn right onto Seventh Street. Make another right onto Fillmore. The Valley Youth Theatre is on the southwest corner of First Street and Fillmore.

PINETOP

CHARLIE CLARK'S STEAKHOUSE

DOES CHARLIE STILL STOP BY?

Home to a most proprietary ghost!

In 1981, when Bill Gibson bought this restaurant that dates back to the 1920s, he knew the structure was once a speakeasy, built by combining two log cabins for the sole purpose of serving moonshine and steaks. What Gibson didn't realize was that a ghost was included in the transaction.

When prohibition ended, the former speakeasy was turned into a restaurant. Charlie Clark purchased the Jake Renfro's Famous Log Cabin Café in 1938 and made it into a steakhouse. Clark's death in 1952 didn't stop him from dropping by from time to time to check on his steakhouse, however. Over the years, though, his "visits" have dwindled.

Gibson used to be the last to leave his restaurant, so before he locked up each evening, he was meticulous about making sure everything was turned off. Which is why he was not at all happy some mornings to find the oven and burners going full blast and the lights on.

He knows old Charlie Clark doesn't mean any harm though. But some employees disagree. Gibson admits that Charlie did go a little too far once. "The Rotary Club was having a meeting in the back bar area," Gibson says, "and the members were saying the Pledge of Allegiance when a picture fell from the wall. It hit a 6-foot-1-inch man standing six feet from the wall with such force that he almost dropped to his knees. Everyone in the room witnessed it, but to this day, no one even mentions the occurrence."

Bartenders have become so spooked that a few of them have left during a shift, Gibson says. A service window, located between the bar and dining area, remains open even after the restaurant is closed for the evening and the bar is still operating. Bartenders have reported seeing through the service window people walking by—even when they know the room is empty and the door padlocked. Music has also been heard coming from the area that was once a dance floor.

Tricia Gibson, Bill's wife, has her own ghost stories. "I was closing down one night in the back bar," she says, "and when I walked past the blender, it turned on by itself. Charlie just wanted me to know that he was still looking after his old restaurant."

Rumors of bootlegging and moonshine at Charlie's Steakhouse are no longer hashed over, but talk about ghosts still runs rampant.

Address:	Charlie Clark's Steakhouse 1701 E. White Mountain Boulevard (Hwy. 260) Pinetop, AZ 85935
Phone:	(928) 367-4900
Hours:	Bar (which also serves lunch) Open: 11 a.m. Dining room opens at 5 p.m.

Directions: From Phoenix: Take I-10 East to US60. Travel through Globe to Show Low. Take SR60 southeast to Pinetop.

PRESCOTT

COYOTE JOE'S
BAR & GRILL

A REAL WORKING GIRL'S GHOST

The old Arizona Hotel, now occupied by Coyote Joe's Bar & Grill, may have been spared from the fire that swept down Montezuma Street in 1900 but it hasn't been spared from its share of ghosts.

Like so many hotels in that era, a brothel was part of the establishment.

Coyote Joe's opened in 1997. Management as well as personnel knew from the start that their building was haunted when one of the managers caught a glimpse of a former employee from the Arizona Hotel. Considering the way the ghost was dressed, there was no doubt about what her profession had been in her previous life. She was in the front area, next to the hostess desk and then floated through the red brick wall that separates the dining room and bar.

Wall between dining room and bar through which the ghost floated.

Although Coyote Joe's other ghosts aren't as bold as the prostitute, they do let themselves be known. "I was surprised one afternoon when I walked upstairs to our banquet area to discover the room was full of smoke," says owner Chad Cornell. "But, it vanished as puzzlingly as it had appeared. The next two times it occurred, I didn't find it as unsettling as that first time. No fire, just smoke billowing about."

Another ghost likes to hang out in the kitchen, once the main room of the brothel. The cooks aren't happy about sharing their space. Apparently when the ghosts are in a spunky mood, they'll often manipulate the stove burners—turning them off while food is still cooking. According to Chad, "In 1991, one of the cooks, after making a rude remark, was whopped on the head by a pan that came flying through the air. Our ghosts are generally not malicious, just feisty and fun."

One of the spirits seems to appreciate how much youngsters like sweets. When Chad's son is with him, before or after business hours, he will sometimes be in the bar area. On one particular morning, he was standing by the M&M candy machine and asked his father if he could please have some candy. As if on cue, the candy machine dropped down some M&M's. Word leaked out, and it wasn't long after that Chad's business partner had candy dispensed to his child as well.

If you need a chocolate fix after enjoying a meal at Coyote Joe's and decide to pass on dessert, try standing by the M&M candy machine and say out loud to your companion, "Could I please have some candy?" Be sure to put your hand under the dispenser, just in case!

Address:	Coyote Joe's Bar & Grill
	214 S. Montezuma St.
	Prescott, AZ 86303
Phone:	(928) 778-9570
Hours:	Bar: 3:00 p.m.-1:00 a.m. daily
	Grill: 3:00 p.m.-11:00 p.m. daily

Directions: From Phoenix: Take I-17 north; exit at Cordes Junction (exit 262) and go west on SR69 into Prescott on SR89. When you reach Montezuma, make a left. Coyote Joe's is on the right-hand side.

PRESCOTT

HASSAYAMPA INN

HE LEFT HER ON THEIR WEDDING NIGHT!

Arrow indicates balcony of Room 406.

When the Hassayampa Inn opened in 1927, it was considered (and still is) Prescott's Grand Hotel. Known as a high-end tourist hotel it was built to attract the summer traveler, especially those living in the Valley of the Sun where sizzling temperatures often soared above 100 degrees. With the arrival of the automobile, people flocked up north seeking cooler weather. In 1928, one young couple decided that the Inn would be the perfect place to spend their wedding night.

Not much is known about the newlywed bride and groom except that her name was Faith. They checked into the Balcony Suite, Room 426, and later that night Faith's husband left the hotel and never returned. Three days later, she hung herself on the balcony overlooking Gurley Street.

The ghost of Faith is responsible for most of the supernatural notoriety of this elegant hotel. Although she does roam about, most occurrences happen in Room 426.

In the fall of 2000, a couple in the Balcony Suite awoke at 3 a.m. to find the water running, the lights on and the radio and television blaring. They wanted to check out right away but after learning the story of Faith, they extended their stay for two more days.

*Balcony Suite, Room 426
and the door to the balcony.*

Another time, an employee was in the hall right outside Faith's room when he heard a loud bang and was astonished when a wreath that was hanging on the door came flying off. The only way that could have happened is if someone had pounded on the door from the inside. The employee checked, of course, but found the room empty.

One entity, known as the "Night Watchman," comes around once a month and rattles all the doors and windows as though checking them to be sure that they are secure.

The one time that Faith was seen was when, out of the corner of his eye, an employee was able to make out that she was wearing a long, pink gown. Is Faith still waiting for her husband to return or is she content to stay alone in this posh hotel?

Address:	Hassayampa Inn 122 E. Gurley Street Prescott, AZ 86301
Phone:	(800) 322-1927

Directions: From Phoenix: Take I-17 North; exit at Cordes Junction (Exit 262) and go west on SR69 and into Prescott on SR89. SR89 turns into Gurley. The Inn is on the corner of Gurley and Marina on the right.

PRESCOTT

PRESCOTT FINE ARTS ASSOCIATION

THE CASE OF THE MISSING CORPSE

Ask anyone in Prescott if they know of any haunted sites and, without a doubt, they'll say the Prescott Fine Arts Association. Father Michael is always mentioned as the culprit, but he isn't the only Roman Catholic priest behind the haunting.

The theater originally was Sacred Heart Church, and the adjacent building, now the administration office, dressing rooms, costume storage and meeting area, was the rectory.

Originally Sacred Heart Church, now the Prescott Fine Arts Theatre.

Fr. Edmond Clossen came to Prescott in 1895 to convert the Indians to Catholicism in the old Arizona territory. Fr. Alfred Quetu invited his fellow priest to stay at Sacred Heart's rectory while he was spreading the Gospel. Father Quetu gave Father Michael, another local priest, the same warm invitation. Both took up the offer to stay.

Seven years later, on June 18 when Father Clossen passed away, the Indians brought back his body for interment. Father Quetu performed the funeral Mass and honored the request for his burial to be underneath the altar.

In the late 1960s, the bishop of the diocese realized that the parish, having outgrown its facilities, needed to build a larger church and rectory elsewhere. Because the old site would no longer be used as a church, a disinterment and reburial of Father Clossen was necessary. When this process began, however, it was discovered that Clossen's remains were gone!

The mystery behind the location of Clossen's corpse remains unsolved.

Today, while theater members prepare for their performances, a persistent noise, like a rattle, can often be heard from Father Michael's old bedroom. The performers rush up to the second floor to try to find the source of the sound, but each time, they find nothing. Are the disturbances Father Michael wanting some company or are they simply the sounds of an aging building?

The altar where Clossen was supposed to have been buried (now used as a stage) is another area where strange things occur. Volunteer Jodi Drake can vouch that there are ghosts there. One evening while Drake was checking the lighting for a graveyard scene, she saw a ghostly shadow glide in front of the painted moon. Unfortunately, she couldn't pinpoint the identity of the silhouette.

Drake wasn't the only one in for a surprise the evening that Noel Coward's play, *Blithe Spirit*, was performed. After the show was over, play director Randy Faulkner and three cast members were setting up bar props for the next day's performance. All of a sudden two glasses jumped up in the air and went crashing to the floor. Ironically, Coward's famous play focuses on a remarried widower, his present wife and the visible ghost of Elvira, the first wife, who delighted in wreaking havoc among the living.

Which priest is responsible for closing opened doors, opening closed doors and turning lights on and off? Father Michael could be held accountable for the rattling that is heard from his bedroom, but are Clossen and Quetu behind the other ghostly activities? And where is Father Clossen's corpse?

Address:	Prescott Fine Arts Association
	208 N. Marina
	Prescott, AZ 86301
Phone:	(928) 445-3286
Hours:	Call for performance times

Directions: From Phoenix: Take I-17 North; exit at Cordes Junction (Exit 262). Go west on SR69 and into Prescott on SR89. Turn right at Marina and go one block. Prescott Fine Arts Association is on your left.

SIERRA
VISTA

DAISY MAE'S STRONGHOLD

GHOST HOST WITH THE MOST

"He's a host, not a ghost" is how Don Willcox, owner of Daisy Mae's, refers to "Charlie," an old cowboy who is in no hurry to leave.

Daisy Mae's building has served Sierra Vista in widely different capacities. Built sometime in the early 1870s as a trading post, the structure subsequently housed a post office, stagecoach stop and, near the turn of the 19th century, a house of ill repute.

According to lore, "Charlie" was stabbed during a fight over a prostitute in 1892 on one of his visits to the brothel. To honor Charlie and his ghost, the room where the tragedy occurred has been named the "Ghost Room."

A previous manager caught sight of Charlie once in a mirror and described him as over six feet tall and very thin with straggly blond hair. After the sighting, the manager refused to come to the restaurant at night. Another employee was in the kitchen preparing meat and caught a glimpse of Charlie's boots out of the corner of her eye. She was so frightened she ran out of Daisy Mae's and never came back.

Willcox doesn't mind the ghost. "I've never seen him although I once saw his shadow going across the wall in the back room. And then there was the time I was working on the bills and the checkbook cover started flipping on its own," Willcox says. "When glasses start to slide across the bar or if a pic-

The Ghost Room, where Charlie died.

ture falls straight off the wall, I just ask him to please stop his shenanigans, and he usually does."

Charlie seems to be more active in the back of the restaurant and in the kitchen. Willcox says he can often hear the ghost mutter but can't make out the words. "He's a very benevolent ghost most of the time. Although, I do think he was responsible for the time that my tool chest went flying off a bar stool."

Female employees aren't as accepting of Charlie as their male counterparts. A common complaint among the waitresses is that they feel like someone is watching them while they're in the restroom. And the servers may have a point: A man resembling Charlie was once "seen" following a female customer into the bathroom. When approached by a staff member, he simply faded away before the startled employee's eyes.

Pam, another waitress, had an unusual experience in the banquet room. Walking around the dining room refilling sugar bowls one afternoon, she felt like she had passed through a spider web. She sensed the same sensation in the area later in the evening. She knew there were no spider webs, but she checked anyway to see what else might have given her the tingling feeling that caused the hairs on her arm to rise up. Finding nothing, Pam blamed it all on Charlie's ghost. When other incidents on her shift occurred, like finding silverware and napkins tossed off the tables, her Charlie theory endured.

When you make dinner reservations, request Charlie's room, and if a tall young man with straggly blond hair saunters close to your table, you can assume his name is Charlie.

Address:	Daisy Mae's Stronghold 332 N. Garden Ave. Sierra Vista, AZ 85635
Phone:	(520) 452-8099
Hours:	4 p.m.-9:30 p.m., Monday-Thursday 4 p.m.-10 p.m., Friday and Saturday 4 p.m.-9 p.m., Sunday

Directions: From Phoenix: Take I-10 East beyond Tucson. Exit at SR90. Travel south to Fry Blvd and turn left. Continue for 1/2 block to Garden Avenue and turn left. Daisy Mae's is on the left.

TEMPE

CASEY MOORE'S OYSTER HOUSE

THE BALLROOM DANCER

William and Mary Moeur, a prominent couple in Tempe, built their Colonial Revival-style home in 1910. Both passed away in the home they loved—William, in front of the fireplace in 1929, and Mary, years later, in her bedroom.

In the 1930s, the building was converted into a boarding house and for a spell, some speculate, it was a bordello. The building was used as a fraternity house before becoming a restaurant named Ninth and Ash in the early 1980s. When Patty St. Vincent purchased the building in 1986, she renovated it and changed the name to Casey Moore's Oyster House.

One spirit who has been seen frequently is described as a lovely woman with long hair who is seen dancing in the upstairs dining room. Some say that it's Mary Moeur, who was always fond of dancing. Dressed in a long, flowing gown, the spirit has been seen by numerous neighbors who have caught glimpses of the apparition gliding past the stained-glass window.

Other neighbors, alarmed that a woman was in Casey's after business hours, have called the police. The sightings have always occurred at 4 a.m., and it doesn't seem to matter that the doors are all locked, with security cameras and alarm systems turned on. Nothing is ever tripped to cause the motion detector to go off. Investigators were eventually able to get an image on one of the security tapes showing the likeness of a woman lingering in the downstairs doorway. The time? Exactly 4 a.m!

Another time, a restaurant worker reported seeing a man and a woman, dressed in 1900s-style clothing, floating up the stairs toward him. He said he could see right through them.

Manager and bartender Maureen Matthews encountered a ghost in 1986. She was getting a glass of wine, and when she turned, a female spirit was standing in front of her. Matthews describes her as

Window where a ghostly ballroom dancer can sometimes be seen.

thin and attractive, with long dark hair and wearing a pastel dress. As soon as their eyes met, Matthews says, the ghost simply vanished.

Each night, employees set tables for the following day. But on more than one occasion, the chairs have been found lined up in the hall, plates moved about and silverware jumbled up in the center of a table. Mary Moeur was too elegant a lady to be responsible for such mayhem, so employees speculate that a more childlike ghost is behind the mischief.

Guests are not exempt from encounters with the playful spirit, either. Gentlemen have reported feeling something tugging at their ties. One customer, enjoying her meal, not only heard "psst" whispered in her ear but felt hot breath as well. A room full of customers once witnessed a picture on a wall go straight up and down before crashing to the floor.

If you'd like to catch a solo performance of a ghostly ballroom dancer, stroll past Casey Moore's at 4:00 a.m. and look up to the second-floor window. But don't call the police. They'll just shrug it off as another normal night on Ash Avenue.

Address:	Casey Moore's Oyster House 850 South Ash Avenue Tempe, AZ 85281
Phone:	(480) 968-9935
Hours:	11 a.m.-1 p.m., daily

Directions: From Phoenix: Take I-10 East and exit onto SR202 towards Tempe. Exit onto SR143 and drive south to University. Drive east on University to Ash and turn right. Casey Moore's is on your right.

TEMPE

MONTI'S LA CASA VIEJA

THIS 'OLD HOUSE'
IS FILLED WITH FINE SPIRITS!

The history behind the oldest remaining building in the Salt River Valley is just as interesting as the ghosts who occupy this 23,000-square-foot rambling steakhouse.

The city of Tempe owes its beginnings to Charles Hayden when he implemented a ferry service across the turbulent Salt River. In 1871, he built a port, which included a blacksmith, carpentry and retail shop. An adobe hacienda served as a residence for him as well as wayfarers in need of a meal or a place to spend the night.

Five years later Hayden married Sallie Calvert Davis, formerly of Arkansas and California. Used to the luxuries of life, Davis was appalled that the floor of her new home was nothing but packed dirt. To please his new bride, Hayden immediately had lumber hauled down from Prescott, making them the first family with wood flooring in the area.

Davis was also disappointed with the spartan Arizona desert, but a friend from California came to her rescue by sending her some grass seed in a cigar box. It wasn't long before her lawn flourished with Bermuda grass.

As was the custom in that era, all three of the Hayden children—Carl, Sallie and Mary—were born at home. Carl, born in 1877, went on to become a soldier, sheriff and U.S. Senator, serving a total of 57 years in Congress.

In 1889, after the family moved to a spacious ranch east of town, their former residence was converted to the Hayden Hotel. There is some speculation that it may have been used as a bordello for a period of time.

Thirty-five years later, the first major renovation of La Casa Vieja occurred when Charles Hayden's daughters, Sallie and Mary, decided to refurbish the deteriorating building to open a tearoom and restaurant. Restoring the structure to its original territorial adobe style, the siblings had the second floor removed. Their new business venture was successful until the stock-market crash of 1929 put them out of business.

The late Leonard Monti purchased the building in 1954, but because it had been vacant and in shabby condition, it wasn't until two years later that Monti's La Casa Vieja was finally opened for business.

In 1992, Monti was quoted in *The Arizona Republic* as saying he felt the ghosts of Charles Trumbull Hayden and his son, Sen. Carl Hayden, roaming the rooms at Monti's. He told the newspaper that when he was alone in the restaurant he could sometimes feel their presences.

"If any place should be haunted, it would be La Casa Vieja," says Michael Monti. "Considering its history and the fact that we have had a few deaths occur in the restaurant—any place where so much human experiences have transpired—it's bound to have a ghost or two."

Michael, the son of Leonard and owner of Monti's La Casa Vieja, hasn't encountered any ghosts himself yet, but his staff is quick to share their experiences with the supernatural.

Judy, a former manager, had a few brushes with the unknown in the 15 years she was employed at Monti's. "While none of my experiences were physically threatening, they were quirky," she says. "One evening only a few of us were in the building and I was on my closing rounds, turning off lights and checking doors. I had just left the Zane Grey Room when I heard three distinct women's voices having a conversation and laughing from within the area I had just left. I peeked in thinking that some employees might be in there but the room was empty and all was quiet. As soon as I left, their conversations started up again."

Monti's La Casa Vieja has at least 27 interior and exterior doors that are wired with security features. One night, after the restaurant had closed, the security system indicated that one of the doors was unsecured so Judy and the bartender went to check on which one needed to be locked up. "We were two steps into the waiting room when the double doors in front of us flew open with a breeze that still gives me chills," Judy says. "Both doors in a full swing, not just a bump, but all the way as if John Wayne, himself, was coming through them."

Perhaps the most unsettling occurrence for Judy was the time an uninvited guest decided to spend the night with her. Walking down the hallway to exit the building, Judy felt a strong presence behind her and felt the hair on the back of her neck go up. The presence stayed with her during her ride home, and, later, while trying to sleep, it was still there. After showering the following morning, she spotted a hard-candy mint on top of her sheet. The candy was the same type kept at the hostess desk at the restaurant, but Judy, who has a sweet tooth for chocolate but not hard candy, never had occasion to keep any of the confections on her person, let alone in her home.

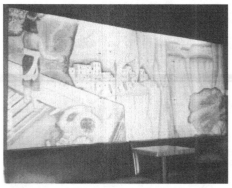
The Mural Room—a tired spirit's refuge?

In 1994 a bus boy, pale and obviously shaken, burst in and sputtered to Monti that he had come across a cowboy in the Mural Room. "He claimed that a cowboy had been relaxing on one of the long padded benches. He insisted that the cowboy, who was wearing boots and a hat, disappeared the minute he glanced away. He was so unnerved, I didn't doubt for a moment his story," Monti says.

The Fountain Room was originally used as an open courtyard when the Hayden sisters operated their tearoom. Now enclosed, it has become a large dining room, with a fountain as its focal point. The cleaning crews say this area must have been a happy place, because they often "hear" the laughter and sounds of children playing in this area.

The Hayden Room, where Carl Hayden was born, also is haunted, according to employees. Sounds of whistling and mysterious noises coming from this large dining room can be unnerving so the crews try to pair up while they clean.

The Fountain Room at Monti's La Casa Vieja.

The late Leonard Monti seems to be still looking over his beloved restaurant. "My dad had a unique way of walking," says Michael, "almost like a shuffling. An employee in the men's restroom once swore he heard Dad's gait outside the door." The restroom is next to Leonard's old office, and banging has been heard coming from the now vacant room.

All the ghosts who wander aimlessly through this 1871 building are content, it seems. But then, who wouldn't be? With more than 23,000 square feet to meander through and employees who leave the ghosts alone, the "old house" is a welcome spot for fine spirits.

Address:	Monti's La Casa Vieja 1 West Rio Salado Parkway Tempe, AZ 85281
Phone:	(480) 967-7594
Hours:	11 a.m.-11 p.m., Sunday-Thursday 11 a.m.-midnight, Friday and Saturday

Directions: From Phoenix: Take I-10 East, exit onto SR202 towards Tempe. Exit south onto Priest, make a left on Rio Salado Parkway. Monti's is on the right at the southwest corner of Mill Avenue & Rio Salado Parkway.

TOMBSTONE

NELLIE CASHMAN'S RESTAURANT

AN ANGEL AMONG US

Nellie Cashman's is the oldest restaurant in "the town too tough to die" and has a reputation for serving the best homemade pies in Tombstone. It may not qualify as the most haunted restaurant in Arizona, but just the same, owners Anita Skinner and her daughter, Sherri, are pretty content with the ghosts they have.

Nellie Cashman was born around 1850 in Ireland and emigrated to the United States 10 years later, settling in Boston. She lived in Nevada and northern British Columbia before settling down in Tombstone in 1880. Cashman operated the Russ House, a boarding house and restaurant, in the same adobe building that now houses the Skinners' restaurant.

The oldest restaurant in town was once owned by the "Angel of Tombstone."

Nicknamed the "Angel of Tombstone," Cashman never turned away a hungry person down on his luck. She frequently turned the Russ House into a clinic, nursing the sick, and was instrumental in founding the first school in Tombstone. She also raised enough funds for construction of the Sacred Heart Catholic Church. Because of all of her charitable work in the community she was respected and loved by all.

In 1923 she moved to Victoria, British Columbia, where she passed away two years later. No one is quite sure if Cashman is one of the ghosts who hang around the restaurant. Says Sherri: "One of our employees mentioned that an older gentleman, dressed in an outdated black suit, walked into the kitchen area one night when he was alone in the building. And late one night I saw a ghost out of the corner of my eye or else I imagined it because I had been up for 12 hours. One of Tombstone's residents did say he saw Nellie coming out of our back door once, carrying a lunch bucket."

Another time, an employee caught sight of a Victorian "lady," again late at night. Still others report lights going on and off and items that move mysteriously or vanish.

There are accounts of ghostly activity that happened before the Skinners took over so they can't be substantiated by Anita or her daughter, but in the world of ghosts, they certainly could be true. A former employee, for example, once witnessed the spirited side of Nellie when a customer made an unflattering remark about her. A jar of mustard sitting in the middle of the table seemed to leap up, spilling the contents all over the customer's dress. An unseen hand would sometimes press down on someone's shoulder and a low voice would call out his or her name. Years ago a waitress left some pans out before locking up and when she returned the next morning different ones were sitting on the stove.

Nellie Cashman, who took so much pride in the Russ House, would be pleased with the restaurant today. If she is one of the ghosts who keep hanging around, you can't blame her. After all, there's no place like home, especially for a spirited woman like Nellie.

Address:	Nellie Cashman's Restaurant 117 S. 5th St. Tombstone, AZ 85638
Phone:	(520) 457-2212

Directions: From Phoenix: Take I-10 East past Tucson to Benson. Go south from Benson on SR80 to Tombstone. The restaurant is two blocks south of Fremont (SR 80) on the corner of 5th and Toughnut.

TOMBSTONE

TOMBSTONE BOARDING HOUSE

THE NOT-SO O.K. CORRAL

Walking by the Tombstone Boarding House, you would never guess that behind the white picket fence lurks an assortment of ghosts. The spirits are as tranquil as the setting so you won't be frightened if you spend the night.

The adobe house, originally known as the Barrows Boarding House, was built in 1880 by

Does Billy Clanton hang around here?

Tombstone's first bank manager and was remodeled and enlarged in the early 1930s. This is where Shirley and Ted Villarin, owners of Tombstone Boarding House, reside. A unique breed of entities occupies their second dwelling, the one you can rent for the night.

A participant in the legendary "gunfight at the O.K. Corral," which occurred on October 16, 1881, Billy Clanton was one of three casualties. One account states that he didn't die of his injuries right away and was whisked away to a nearby building. Could it have been the White Room in the Barrows Boarding House where he screamed in agony until he was given morphine? Although the medicine calmed him down, his heart gave way before any other treatment could be administered.

Shirley relates two incidents that have occurred in the White Room. "A young couple always requests this room in hopes of an encounter with Billy. On their third visit they happily reported over breakfast that they saw him. My secretary just couldn't resist. She dashed off to the White Room and returned very excited with the news that she had seen him very clearly in the bathroom."

On another occasion, "A close friend of mine spent the night," Shirley says, "and spotted a young blond-haired man. She also felt the presence of a young woman who was begging the gentleman not to go to the window or door. She sensed that there was an angry crowd outside, ready to lynch him."

The Green Room is the perfect place for anyone who welcomes dreams. Two women spent the night there once—several weeks apart – and experienced the same, vivid dream. The two guests independently reported that a young woman dressed in Victorian attire and a man wearing a duster and Western hat walked through their room. The dream ended with the couple continuing through the door and into a garden that was covered by a trellis with climbing roses.

During the filming of a movie, *Ghosts of Tombstone*, producers stayed in the Gold Room and got some special effects that weren't in the script. In the middle of the night, they were awakened to the sound of someone walking. But much to their dismay, there wasn't anyone around who could be held accountable for the mysterious footsteps.

Two ghosts have also been spotted by a guest in the main house— the apparition of a mother and what looked like her daughter, polishing furniture in the family room.

There are several rooms to choose from if you want to try to mingle with the spirits at the Tombstone Boarding House. But if you'd like some help with your housework, try to convince Shirley to allow you to throw down a sleeping bag in her family room in hopes that mother and daughter will follow you home!

Address:	Tombstone Boarding House
	108 N. Fourth Street
	Tombstone, AZ 85638
Phone:	(520) 457-3716

Directions: From Phoenix: Take I-10 East past Tucson to Benson. Go south from Benson on SR80 to Tombstone. Turn left off of SR80 (Fremont Street) at Fourth Street. The Tombstone Boarding House is located at the corner of Fourth and Safford streets on the right.

TUBAC

TUBAC GOLF RESORT

WHEN JOHNNY COMES MARCHING HOME AGAIN

If you come to this resort to tee-off, don't worry about the ghost!

The resort property dates back to 1789 when Don Toribio de Otero of Northern Sonora received the first Arizona land grant from the King of Spain. This "gift" encompassed what is now Tubac and much of the surrounding areas.

Many of the old structures from the original stables, haylofts and bunkhouse are still in use today. The adobe walls in the dining room and lounge are from the original ranch, also home to a ghost the staff call "Johnny."

Not much is known about Johnny except that he is a little boy with blond hair and is always dressed in short pants. Like any child, he can be bratty at times.

Johnny doesn't seem to have a favorite area of the resort. Some days, he shows up in the kitchen, much to the dismay of workers. While on KP, Johnny likes to fiddle with the electrical appliances, especially the microwave, which he constantly turns on and off. He also toys with the coffee maker. The staff always holds their breath when they arrive in the morning, wondering if they are going to find a pile of broken dishes to sweep up, thanks, they say, to Johnny.

Reservations staff aren't happy, either, when Johnny comes marching in, because he can do havoc in their small office space. Staplers and Scotch tape turn up missing, and, at times, he takes it upon himself to scatter office supplies and paperwork on the floor.

When he isn't being a holy terror, the staff agrees, Johnny can be a very pleasant little fellow to have around. As soon as he learns your name, he'll call it out, and you can often hear the happy thud of his ball when he's bouncing it in the banquet room. And like most ghosts, he closes doors that have been opened. One always knows when he is about by the sound of his tiny footsteps.

The Tubac Golf Resort is open to the public and only minutes away from the town of Tubac. Several residents in this artistic community also claim they have ghosts that live side by side with them. One retired couple has a ghost who threw a sock that had been missing for two weeks, at their shower door. Another family thinks their ghost must be a child because they can hear marbles rolling across their floor. A third family complains that books simply drop off their bookshelves. The town itself has the honor of hosting its own ghost, known as the Ghost of Tubac. A 4-foot-tall female ghost, she strolls along the railroad tracks outside the city.

If you come to this resort to tee-off, don't worry about distractions from Johnny. He seems content to stay within the boundaries of the main building.

Address:	Tubac Golf Resort
	1 Otero Road (P.O. Box 1297)
	Tubac, AZ 85646
Phone:	(520) 398-2211

Directions: Take I-10 East; just south of Tucson, exit onto I-19. Drive south to Exit 40 (Chavez Siding Road). Go south three miles.

TUCSON

HOTEL CONGRESS

A CRIME STORY __AND__ A GHOST TALE

For true-crime buffs, who are fascinated with ghostly phenomena as well, it doesn't get much better than the Hotel Congress. Though there is no connection between Public Enemy No. 1's escape from the hotel and the ghosts who inhabit here, both stories must be told:

John Dillinger and his gang traveled to Tucson in the winter of 1934 to lay low from the authorities back East. Using aliases, the men were on the third floor of the 1919 hotel when a fire broke out. The men blew their cover when Russell Clark, one of the gang members, offered a large tip to two firemen if they would return to the burning building to retrieve their gun-laden bags from the flames.

Recognized by one of the firemen who had seen photos of Dillinger and some of his men in *True Detective Magazine*, the gang was identified to the police. A stakeout ensued and Dillinger was tracked to a house nearby where he was apprehended. Soon the other three men, all on the FBI's "Most Wanted List," were captured. They were all extradited to Crown Point, Indiana and placed in the county jail. A month later, Dillinger escaped by using a pistol carved from an old washboard that he had blackened with boot polish.

Shana and Richard Oseran purchased this historic hotel in 1985, renovating and refurbishing it in late-19th-century style. In addition to its beautiful décor, ghost stories and legends here keep the past alive.

The ghost of a man with the initials T.S. is often seen on the second floor. Apparently, the man had died in a gunfight that arose from an argument over a card game in the lobby of the Congress. T.S. had caught his opponent cheating and was killed in the resulting altercation. As a ghost, he always wears an old-fashioned gray suit and is frequently seen peering out the windows of the upper floor.

Staircase where the ghost of a Victorian lady is seen

A female ghost who dresses in Victorian clothing is probably the most frequently spotted ghost. She is always reported "seen" on the stairwell or in the lobby. There is also a distinctive scent of roses associated with her sightings.

A desk clerk once saw her slowly descend the staircase into the lobby. Not the least bit shy or withdrawn, the ghost seemed to enjoy being in the limelight.

Lastly, there is the hotel's beloved, longest-staying permanent resident, Vince. He lived in the hotel for 36 years, and since his death in 2001, employees have been finding butter knives from the hotel's Cup Café in different locations on the second floor. Vince was known to constantly carry a butter knife, which he would use as a screwdriver.

When you visit the Hotel Congress be sure to spend some time in the open lounge area on the second floor. There is a large display of memorabilia on John Dillinger there. The staff at the Hotel Congress would appreciate you returning any butter knives you find!

Address: Hotel Congress
311 E. Congress Street
Tucson, AZ 85701

Phone: (800) 722-8848

Directions: From Phoenix: Take I-10 East to Tucson. Take Congress Street exit (Exit 259). Go east onto Congress Street. The hotel will be on the left.

TUCSON

LI'L ABNER'S STEAKHOUSE

THINGS GO BETTER
WITH COCA-COLA!

Is the former owner who stops by for a Coke the only ghost here?

Customers always tell the staff at Li'l Abner's how much they enjoyed their meal, but so far have said not a morsel about the sighting of a ghost. Could that be because "George" is only comfortable around the staff, too shy to make his presence known to diners?

This adobe dwelling started out as a Butterfield Express stage stop in the early 1800s and for a long period of time, housed an eyeglass factory. Li'l Abner's opened up as a restaurant and bar in 1947.

Considering the history of the building, one would expect that George might be an old cowpoke or an outlaw. Instead, Li'l Abner's ghost is said to be the former maintenance man who passed away in the 1990s.

Wardell works the early shift at Li'l Abner's, preparing pinto beans for the evening's hungry customers. "Whenever George would take a drive to Mexico, he always stopped at the bar for a large glass of Coke," Wardell explains. "After he passed away, I saw him standing next to the bar, all dressed in white, drinking his Coke. And then, he disappeared. He must have been making another trip to Mexico."

Wardell also says he hears unusual sounds coming from George's old room. George was known to have a love of Cap'n Crunch cereal, so many here believe the crunching sound is old George having a snack.

Wardell isn't the only one who has experienced the paranormal in the bar area. Shawn Bell, the bar's manager, has heard things falling behind the bar, and on numerous occasions has heard someone call out his name. When he turns around, Bell finds that he is the only one there.

Some employees feel that the entire building is haunted. Muffled conversations and loud knocking on doors are not uncommon. When staff members try to track down the source of the noises, they come up empty.

There has also been speculation that a spirit belonging to one of the factory workers from the original eyeglass plant is still looking for a mislaid pair of spectacles. Could he be the one knocking on the various doors, disturbing employees at Li'l Abner's? If so, to whom is he talking?

As long as these ghosts stay away from the outdoor mesquite-burning fire pit, the cooks are happy. They don't need help from a factory worker who can't see without his glasses.

Address:	Li'l Abner's Steakhouse 8500 N. Silverbell Road Tucson, AZ 85743
Phone:	(520) 744-2800
Hours:	5 p.m.-10 p.m., Sunday-Thursday 5 p.m.-11 p.m., Friday and Saturday

Directions: From Phoenix: Take I-10 East to Tucson. As you are approaching Tucson, take the Ina Road exit (#248). Turn right (west) onto Ina Road and then turn north on Silverbell Road. Lil' Abner's Steakhouse will be on the left.

UNIVERSITY OF ARIZONA'S CENTENNIAL HALL

THE MAN IN BLACK

Centennial Hall's other ghost is a female. Once, "out of the corner of my eye," Kennedy says, she caught a fleeting glance of the spirit in a sheer-green, billowing dress while Kennedy was working in the Green Room. "And I heard her early one Sunday morning when I came in to get something I had forgotten," she adds. "As I walked from the back-stage area to the lobby, I suddenly heard a woman talking to someone. I knew there weren't any custodians on the premises since we didn't have a show the previous evening. I walked to where the chattering seemed to be coming from but as soon as I was within 50 feet to where I heard the voice, the conversation stopped."

According to maintenance workers, most of the action takes place, appropriately enough, on the graveyard shift. Custodians say they've heard the piano play when no one is around, the wails of a woman coming from the main house area, and, in one odd instance, something that sounded like a horse's whinny coming from the stage.

After arriving one morning, Kennedy ran into a sub-janitor who'd just finished his shift. "His eyes were huge, and as he left, he

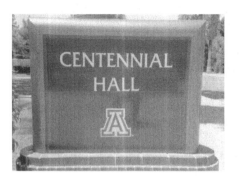

Who are the other "per-formers" here?

claimed he'd never work here again. He didn't say why, but he looked so unnerved, I figured our 'friends' must have been up to some mischief," she says.

Kennedy is never afraid to be alone in the hall even though she's encountered a touch of the supernatural. To her, the theater is a wonderful place to be—the perfect spot for spirits.

Address:	University of Arizona's Centennial Hall 1020 E. University Blvd. Tucson, AZ 85721
Phone:	(520) 621-3341
Hours:	Call for performance times

Directions: From Phoenix: Take I-10 East to Tucson. Exit at St. Mary's Road (Exit 257A) and go left (east). St. Mary's Road becomes 6th Street. Continue until you reach Park. Make a left on Park, turning right at University. Centennial Hall is the second building on your right.

VAIL

COLOSSAL CAVE

A SPELUNKING SPIRIT!

Just northeast of Tucson, Colossal Cave is an exciting place to visit.

The Colossal Cave has countless connecting rooms and rock formations resembling waterfalls, animals, people and even elves. It's an ideal hiding place for outlaws on the lam, and the perfect setting for a ghost story.

In 1887 three such outlaws robbed a train of $3,000 and decided that the Colossal Cave would be a good hideout. A 31-man posse guarded the entrance for two weeks and tried smoking them out, but the bandidos escaped from another exit. The loot was never recovered but plenty of evidence was left behind. Empty bags, bullet-shell casings, blankets, utensils and clothing were found in the back recesses of the caverns.

The ghosts are few and far between at the Colossal Cave but all it takes is one to attain the title of "haunted."

Only one female ghost has been seen but she hasn't been around for years. Simply called the "Lady in White," she was once a regular visitor, both inside the cave and by the entrance. No one knows who she was, why she picked the cave as her home or why she left so abruptly.

Does Frank Schmidt still "tour" Colossal Cave?

One apparition that still appears resembles the late Frank Schmidt, who was instrumental in developing the Colossal Cave as it is today. "Pop," as he was sometimes called, was a German immigrant who came to Tucson in 1917. He was lured to the cave after hearing the various stories surrounding it, and in 1922 he filed two mining claims on land occupied by the cave. He started offering tours the following year, outfitting his intrepid guests with ropes and lanterns and leading them through the unimproved passageways. In 1934, Schmidt relinquished his leases to the state of Arizona. "Pop" operated the Colossal Cave, personally or through managers, until the age of 84, then died a year later.

Once, a former tour guide was leading a group out of the Lower River Passage when he noticed an image of an older, thin man sitting on a step by the Silent Waterfall. When he was shown a photo of a group shot, he picked Frank Schmidt as the ghost he had seen perched on the steps.

A few years later, "Pop" was once again spotted, this time in the cave "Living Room." A woman who was on a tour wanted to know if the guide was going to wait for "that older gentleman back there." When the guide glanced back he didn't see anyone, but the visitor swore that there was a slight, older man wearing a plaid flannel shirt, just sitting on the stairs. When they were done with the tour, the woman proceeded to a nearby bulletin board where she immediately recognized the picture of the elderly man who had been lagging behind. The man she pointed out to the tour guide was Mr. Frank Schmidt.

Another legend linked to the cave follows a young Indian girl who was trying to escape from a bear. The original entrance was only a 2-foot-round circle, and the girl crawled in, not realizing that it was a straight fall of 12 feet to the cave floor. The story goes that she was never seen again.

Don Kiefer, former tour guide and author of *Haunts of Arizona*, points out in his book that guests on his tours often mentioned hearing the cries of a young woman. The sobs were always reported as having come from the Lower River Passage, which, coincidently, was the same location from which another tour guide had heard a woman either crying or singing.

Is there any truth to the story abut the Indian maiden falling to her death? If so, maybe she is the one weeping. If it's only folklore, then who is this mysterious woman and why is she so prone to crying spells?

Address:	Colossal Cave Mountain Park
	16711 Colossal Cave Road
	Vail, Arizona 85641
Phone:	(520) 647-7275
Hours:	September 16-March 15:
	9 a.m.-5 p.m., Monday-Saturday
	9 a.m.-6 p.m., Sundays and holidays
	March 16-September 15:
	8 a.m.-6 p.m., Monday-Saturday
	8 a.m.-7 p.m., Sundays and holidays

Directions: From Phoenix: Take I-10 East to Tucson. Continue east to Vail-Wentworth Exit (#279). Go north seven miles to Colossal Cave Mountain Park.

WICKENBURG

VULTURE CITY

A HEAVY 'LODE'
FOR THESE GHOSTS!

Vulture City was once the third largest community in the territory.

Driving toward the old mining camp of Vulture City, one knows right away this authentic "ghost town" isn't a place for city slickers. There aren't any staged gunfights or dance-hall girls parading down Main Street. The shops don't sell overpriced Western shirts and sunglasses. You won't find a cowboy steakhouse here either. What you will find are relics of the old West—rusted mining equipment and crumbling old structures; antique furniture and tools; dusty threadbare clothing and worn-out old boots; and lots of pots and pans.

Immigrant Henry Wickenburg found himself in Arizona around 1862 searching for gold. His discovery at Vulture Mine a year later brought hundreds of people to the area, making Vulture City the third largest community in the territory. At its peak, the town had a population of 5,000.

Vulture City should have a line-up of spirits considering all the violent deaths that happened here.

The mine itself claimed seven men in 1923. While the men were pilfering gold, pillars collapsed on them, entombing them along with 12 burros. Their bodies are still buried deep in the sunken lode.

The Vulture City hanging tree near Henry Wickenburg's cabin.

The hanging tree, beside Henry Wickenburg's cabin, was used mainly for men found guilty of rape and murder, but 18 thieves were hung there, too, according to legend, after they were caught stealing gold ore from the mine.

Mine Manager John Osborne says with that kind of history, the place is bound to be spooked: "Several psychics have been to Vulture City and told me that there is quite a bit of supernatural phenomena going on," he says. "One time, seven of us, including a psychic, were sitting in a circle in our living room and we all heard very distinct footsteps from another part of the house. It's not uncommon at all to pick up sounds of a party going on towards the main part of Vulture City."

The mess hall, apparently, is pretty messy, too. "Marge, my wife, has mentioned that at times when she has traipsed past the old mess hall, she can smell a cake baking," Osborne says.

Could ghostly cooks still be using this stove?

Another time, Osborne adds, Russ Hunting, a resident for several years, was in the process of cleaning out the mess hall, when an eerie silence came over him. "Suddenly, shouts of approval came from out of nowhere," Osborne says, "like they were cheering him on, telling him he was doing a good job. Eventually, the voices faded away, the silence wasn't as intense and his hearing slowly came back to normal."

Two houses, dating back to the early 1890s, are perched on the hill above the mine. Both of them were used by the mine owners and both are haunted, according to John and Marge, who live in the larger house.

"A few years ago I was asleep in the bedroom and I woke up, looked into the living room and saw a man standing there. He was well dressed, had on a shirt and tie and was a very distinguished-looking older gentleman. He startled me but before I could say anything, he was gone. I blinked my eyes a few times and looked all around, but there was no one there."

Another time, he adds, "I was driving up the hill and I saw Marge standing in the front door of the house. I parked the car and went inside but couldn't find her. I looked in all of the rooms and I even walked around the outside of the house, but I couldn't find her anywhere. Come to find out, she had been visiting my brother's wife all afternoon. I don't know what I saw standing in the doorway of our house that afternoon. I definitely saw something, but it couldn't have been Marge."

Although John and Marge's home isn't open to the public, there are plenty of other places in Vulture City where apparitions have been seen. The hanging tree, perhaps?

Address:	Vulture City 36610 N. 355th Ave. (mailing address only) Wickenburg, AZ 85390
Phone:	(602) 859-2743
Hours:	Self guided Tours: Summer: Fri, Sat, Sun—8:00-4:00 Winter: 7 days a week—8:00-4:00
Fee:	$7 Adults, $6 Senior discount, $5 for children 6-12.
Directions:	From Phoenix: Take US89/60 (Grand Ave.) to Wickenburg. Go west on US60 about three miles. Go south 12 miles on Vulture Mine Road.

FARAWAY RANCH

THIS GHOST SHAKES...AND BAKES!

Faraway Ranch in the Chiricahua National Monument.

Faraway Ranch is unusual in that the two spirits that watch over the property are a mother and her daughter.

In 1888, Emma and Neil Erickson homesteaded with a small cabin in remote Bonita Canyon. The young Swedish couple enlarged their small cabin nine years later when the family, now consisting of their children, Lillian, Hildegarde and Lewis, needed larger quarters.

When daughter Lillian married Ed Riggs in 1923, the young couple decided to modernize and expand the cabin belonging to her parents and turn it into a guest resort. Lilly promised "good horses and guides for the guests...thrills of cowboy life...a real ranch" in the brochures and advertisements she used in their promotion. Thus was born the Faraway Ranch, a huge success that brought guests back year after year. Lillian entertained her guests with stories of the frontier days, played the piano in the evenings and showed off her horsemanship by accompanying many guests on their trail rides. She was also known to be a wonderful cook, especially for her mouthwatering pies.

Neil and Emma both stayed on at Faraway Ranch until their deaths. Ed Riggs died in 1950, but Lillian, who at the time of her demise was both blind and deaf, lived until 1977.

In 1979 the National Park Service purchased the ranch and later opened it to the public. At a 1990s Park Service open house, a friend of Lillian's was asked if she thought Emma would have had a good time at the party. The reply was: "But she's here with us, having a wonderful time. I can smell her perfume!"

Emma Erickson's favorite possession was her Bible that is on display. An expert explained to the staff that the spine of the Bible is fragile. It's best to turn the pages on a regular basis, she told them. But the ghost of Emma isn't cooperating with that recommendation. Park Ranger Jan Ryan checks the pages of Emma's Bible frequently and always finds it opened to the ghost-woman's favorite page of scripture.

Late one evening, the alarm at the Faraway Ranch went off, and a law-enforcement officer rushed over, sure someone had broken in. Fortunately, he didn't find anyone but he related to Park Ranger and museum curator Kathrine Neilsen that as soon as he walked in, it was as if he had just entered a bakery. The aroma of baked goods was intense as he searched the ranch, looking for the source that triggered the alarm.

In 2000, a historian from Willcox visited the Faraway Ranch. "Whiffs of Lillian's famous pies were so prevalent," she said, "you would have thought she was in the kitchen taking them out of the oven."

Not only will you be amazed at the beauty of the Chiricahua Mountains that surround the Faraway Ranch, you'll be equally amazed when you learn that, although the ranch smells like a bakery, there's not a pie or cake on site.

Address:	Chiricahua National Monument
	13063 E. Bonita Canyon Road
	Willcox, AZ 85643
Phone:	(520) 824-3560
Hours:	The Monument is open 8:00am-5:pm daily. Closed Christmas. Tours of Faraway Ranch: Sat. at 2:00pm.
Directions:	From Phoenix: Take I-10 East past Tucson and continue on to Willcox. Take SR186 south to the Monument.

REX ALLEN MUSEUM and the WILLCOX COWBOY HALL OF FAME

THIS COWBOY JUST CAN'T STOP SINGIN'!

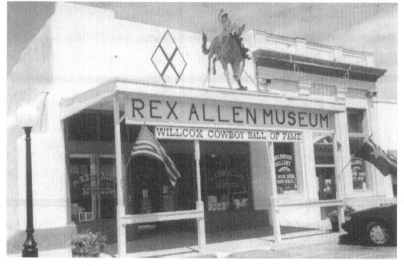

Photo by Kate Dobson Hunt

In a building that once housed the rowdy Schley Saloon, you would think that the original owner, Josef Schwertner, and a sloshed cowboy still looking for a shot of whiskey, would be behind the ghostly activities. Instead, two other ghosts—one quite famous, the other quite unknown—are the culprits.

Operating from 1897 to 1919 as a tavern—until prohibition forced a change to the grocery business, the building housing the Rex Allen Museum and Willcox Cowboy Hall of Fame is one of the town's oldest. Divided into two parts, the facility's first area illustrates the life history of Allen, beginning with his childhood in Willcox and following through to his film and music career. Western and personal memorabilia as well as the late cowboy performer's suits, boots and saddles are displayed throughout.

The second area of the museum pays tribute to respected individuals in the region's cattle industry. Historic photographs provide an interesting contrast between the real-life working cowboys and ranchers and how they were depicted in cinema.

Rex Allen Days, the first weekend of October, is an annual event honoring the late singer, started in 1951. In 2000, Rex Allen Jr. was on stage, and before telling a joke, admitted that his father would probably disapprove of the off-color humor he was about to share. He was right on target; the moment Jr. began, his guitar strap broke.

That same year, while in the museum, Allen's daughter-in-law happened to glance up just when a fragile teacup toppled over on its own. Museum volunteers also reported seeing the back door unlock on its own.

Kate Dobson-Hunt, a close friend of the silver-screen cowboy, shared this experience: "It was about 6:30 p.m. when I happened to walk by and heard one of Rex's songs playing from the outdoor speakers of the museum. No one was in the building to turn on the music, which stopped as suddenly as it started. It was just Rex's way of letting me know he's still around."

Dobson-Hunt had another, even more startling, experience once. Returning from the back of the museum one day, she saw a ghost, totally relaxed, leaning on a saddle that was on display.

Across the street from the Rex Allen Museum, is a larger-than-life bronze sculpture of Allen. The well-known singer passed away on December 17, 1999, and at his request, his ashes were scattered at this small park. It's not surprising to the residents of Willcox that his presence is often felt there. After all, he never forgot his roots.

Address:	The Rex Allen Museum/Willcox Cowboy Hall of Fame 150 N. Railroad Avenue Willcox, AZ 85643
Phone:	(520) 384-4583
Hours:	10 a.m.-4 p.m, daily, except for Thanksgiving

Directions: From Phoenix: Take I-10 East past Tucson towards Willcox. Take Business Loop I-10 (Exit 336) to Willcox's first stoplight. Turn east and go one block. Turn left on to Railroad Avenue. The museum is on the left side of the street.

WILLIAMS

THE RED GARTER
BED & BAKERY

PROSTITUTE OR POLTERGEIST?

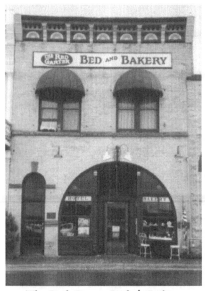

*The Red Garter Bed & Bakery,
is on the famous Route 66.*

John Holst can't guarantee a sighting of the ghost he calls "Eve." After all, she is very shy, he says, appearing to only a select few.

The restored late-19th-century building provides a peek at an earlier time when prostitution was in full swing. The bordello, which had its own private entrance, was located on the second floor, and a saloon on the first. Over the years it also featured a Chinese restaurant and an opium den. During the Dust Bowl years it was a flophouse for travelers on Route 66.

When Holst purchased the former house of ill repute in 1979, he had his hands full. It took him 15 years to restore the Red Garter Bed and Bakery to its original grandeur. The eight "cribs" and central parlor were converted into four large guest rooms, and the former saloon serves as bakery, café and lobby.

So much history has been made at the Red Garter, it's not surprising that ghostly activity occurs. Many nights Holst hears heavy doors solidly close after he has locked up for the night. And one time, while alone in the house, he heard a loud, heretofore unexplained "clunk," similar to a heavy lid falling.

Nightlights line the stairway and come on when motion detectors are triggered by movement. For no apparent reason, however, they sometimes flicker on and off, as though someone were moving up the steps. After replacing them—twice!—Holst swears it's not just a gadget glitch. Something (or someone) is causing the lights to blink.

Perhaps there is a reason that eerie noises, footsteps and flickering nightlights occur on the narrow stairs leading to the former bordello. A prostitute once stabbed one of her clients, the legend goes, causing him to fall down the stairs, through the front door. He subsequently died in the street. Is it the victim or the fallen angel still reliving that night long ago?

This 1934 photo shows saloon owner Longino Mora with the madam of the bordello above his saloon. She is dressed up for the tourists on a rodeo weekend. Longino married five times, fathered 25 children and lived to be 90 years old!

Photo courtesy of Carmina Saggau

In this photograph, Longino Mora is standing with a group of people in front of the bar. Notice the woman standing in the back close to the counter. The woman, who is the only one smiling, casts no reflection in the mirror that she is posed in front of!

It is "Eve" that has even the self-described "hard-core skeptic" Holst admitting that there just may be something to all this ghost business. He now readily admits she's part of the Red Garter reputation: "She usually stays upstairs in the Best Gal's Room, where the top-of-the-line girls would lean out the window to wave in customers. She likes to wake up guests by pushing slightly down on their mattresses and is also known for leaving butterfly kisses on the arms of unsuspecting visitors."

Red Garter employee Alberto Trejo and his nieces were lucky enough once to catch a glimpse of the young woman going from room to room. Trejo described her as a young woman with Hispanic features and long dark hair. She was garbed in a long, white, flowing nightgown. A few other guests have reported "seeing" Eve in their dreams. The description they gave their host resembled the girl that Trejo encountered upstairs.

It took Eve a few years before she made an appearance, so by now two or three spirits may have come out of hiding as well. Hopefully, they'll have her low-key personality as well.

Address:	The Red Garter Bed and Bakery 137 W. Railroad Avenue Williams, AZ 86046
Phone:	(800) 328-1484
Hours:	7 a.m.-11 a.m and 4 p.m.-8 p.m daily Closed: The day after Thanksgiving. Open again on Valentine's Day.

Directions: From Phoenix: Take I-17 North to Flagstaff. Exit onto I-40 West. Enter Williams at Exit 165, following Old Route 66 (Railroad Avenue, which is one way) to the Red Garter Bed and Bakery.

ROD'S STEAK HOUSE

RODNEY'S DANGER FIELD

You can't miss Rod's Steak House in Williams!

Since Route 66 became the main street of America, restaurants, diners and cafes have come and gone. But Rod's Steak House, located right on the Mother Road, has been continuously serving its customers since 1946.

Rodney and Helen Graves established this historic landmark. Rod Graves who, they say, was "married" to his business, passed away in his office the day after his restaurant was sold in 1967. Even in death, however, the devoted restaurateur must still feel married to his old steakhouse, because he is still very much a presence here.

When the third owners, Lawrence and Stella Sanchez, purchased Rod's in 1985, little did they know how much Grave's spirit would test them in their first year of operation.

"It was pretty hectic that first year," says Steve, a waiter. "Close to the area where Rod's office had been, a large mirror shattered from the inside out. It was almost as if someone had knocked the glass *outward*. (Other times) photos would fall right off the wall."

When the late Rod Graves realized how well the Sanchezes kept up the place, things started settling down.

In fact, Lawrence Sanchez gives full credit to Rod for locating a ring he'd once lost and had no hope of finding. After weeks of searching, Lawrence came to work one day and found the ring sitting right on top of a copy machine.

"Shortly after I started working here, I had my first experience with the restaurant's ghost," Steve says. "I heard very distinct footsteps behind me—on a carpeted floor! And I could feel a very strong presence, but when I turned around, I found myself alone in the room. Immediately the hairs on my neck and arm stood straight up. Another time, right after I had served the ladies from a local bridge club, as I turned and walked away, I could feel a presence in back of me. He continued following me all the way downstairs."

The next time you're in Williams, be sure and get your kicks on Route 66 by stopping in at Rod's Steak House. It's not hard to find. Just keep your eyes open for Domino, a huge fiberglass steer that sits by the front entrance. There's no missing the steer that's perched on the roof either.

Address:	Rod's Steak House
	301 E. Route 66 (Bill Williams Ave.)
	Williams, AZ 86046
Phone:	(928) 635-2671
Hours:	11:30a.m.-9:30 p.m., daily

Directions: From Phoenix: Take I-17 North to Flagstaff. Exit onto I-40 West. Enter Williams at Exit 165, turn left, following Old Route 66 (Railroad Avenue). This is a one-way road but if you pass up Rod's just keep on going. It will circle around to Rod's other side and become Bill Williams Avenue. The restaurant stretches for a block between Bill Williams and Railroad avenues.

WILLIAMS DEPOT

HAVE YOUR (HARVEY) GIRL
CALL MY (HARVEY) GIRL!

You can take a trip to the Grand Canyon,
or into the past at the Williams Depot.

Your journey on the historic 1923 Pullman coach car will snake through prairie and lush countryside before reaching the South Rim of the Grand Canyon. The Williams Depot, where you will board, was built in 1908 as the Fray Marcos Hotel and Depot. And like so many other railroad depots throughout the United States, the Fred Harvey system provided restaurant and hotel services. Staffed mostly by the famous "Harvey Girls," the young women were paid well and received free room and board. They were known by their uniform, which consisted of a black dress that fell to just above the ankle and a crisp, white apron.

The Williams Depot is now home to the ticket counter for the famous Grand Canyon Railway, a gift shop and a railroad museum. It's also the spirit home to at least two Harvey Girls and one gentleman (at least the staff thinks it's a gentleman) who loves to whistle.

Mary Tobin, a clerk who worked at the Williams Depot for five years, had her initial experience with one of the girls only a few months after she started working.

"I saw a young woman floating about three feet off the floor by the back door, close to the ticket counter," Tobin says. "She was very beautiful, dressed in white and looked almost spiritual, very pure. She was taller than most women from the early 1900s and she resembled one of the Harvey Girls in an old photo. Unfortunately, she wasn't identified so I don't know who she was."

Tobin, however, was able to match a name to the face of the second ghost – "Clara." The museum has photos of four Harvey Girls that date back to the early 1900s. The first time Tobin encountered that ghost with the "feisty personality," she immediately referred to the photo and recognized her.

"She looks exactly like the Harvey Girl that was wearing glasses. She appeared to be about 4-foot-11," Tobin adds. "I saw her about four or five times in different areas of the building and I would always bid her good night before leaving the building."

Tobin is correct when she describes Clara as "feisty." Giftshop clerks attribute all manner of strange goings-on to Clara. They have seen cookbooks and other items fly off the shelves. And, apparently, Clara's ghost loves an audience: When she tosses T-shirts from the neatly folded stacks of clothing in the gift shop, customers, not wanting to be blamed for the havoc, throw their arms up in the air, declaring to anyone who will listen, that they didn't touch a thing.

While on the second floor digging out holiday decorations, a maintenance man once found himself scurrying down the steps when he heard whistling next to him. He returned a short time later, but the minute the whistling started again, he headed straight back down.

This may be the only Harvey House that still has its girls, with their freshly starched aprons, still on the premises.

Address: Williams Depot
233 N. Grand Canyon Blvd.
Williams, AZ 86046

Phone: (800) 843-8724

Hours: 8 a.m.-6:30 p.m.

Directions: From Phoenix: Take I-17 North to Flagstaff. Exit onto I-40 West. Enter Williams at Exit 163; follow Grand Canyon Blvd. one-half mile south.

WINSLOW

BO JO'S GRILL & SPORTS CLUB

DON'T BE AFRAID...
IT'S ONLY 'GRANDPA'!

Bruchman's Trading Post opened in 1914 and continued in that capacity until 1995 when it became a restaurant.

The ghost at Bo Jo's has never been "seen" but there's no denying who it is. "The cigar aroma gives away his identity," laughs owner Jeannie Jacobs.

"Mr. Bruchman, proprietor of Bruchman's Trading Post, was known to smoke cigars when he was in his office. The cigar aroma originates from that area. Everyone around here calls him Grandpa because that's who he reminds you of—a nice, pleasant grand-fatherly type."

Bruchman's signage.

Jeannie and John live above the restaurant, and one Sunday, after Bo Jo's was closed for the day, Jeannie was on the phone with her sister. During the conversation, she heard the ding of the waitress bell. As soon as she mentioned what she had just heard, the ding sounded again.

Another time, Jeannie says, "I was awakened with a jolt by the dishwasher going on and off. At first I thought nothing of it as I assumed that my grandmother was in the kitchen. But when I went downstairs there wasn't anyone there. I checked the clock and when I realized that it was 4:30 a.m. I really knew then that it couldn't be my grandma.

"While I was alone in the building one (other) afternoon I heard someone whisper 'hello' in my ear. The hair on my neck immediately stood on end and I went icy cold," Jeannie says. "I assumed it was Grandpa letting me know he was around."

Bo Jo's, once an old trading post.

The Jacobs do not feel threatened in any way by their gentleman ghost. To them he's their protector, looking after them and their business.

Gone are the days when you could purchase Indian jewelry, crafts and souvenirs from Bruchman's. Instead you can have a good meal in an old trading post and, if you're lucky, the presence of the former owner.

Address:	Bo Jo's Grill & Sports Club 117 W. 2nd Street Winslow, AZ 86047
Phone:	(928) 289-0616
Hours:	11:00am – 9pm daily

Directions: From Phoenix: Take I-17 North to Flagstaff. Take I-40 East to Winslow; take Exit 252 going into Winslow. This is a one-way street that turns into 2nd Street. Bo Jo's will be on the right.

WINSLOW

RIALTO THEATER

THEATER OF THE ABSURD!

The Rialto Theater is scheduled to reopen in 2002.

Originally built as an opera house, the Rialto Theater has a surplus of ghost stories. Everyone loves a good ghost story, especially residents of Winslow.

One of the old managers of the Rialto who lived there for 20 years told some of his stories to current owner Allan Affeldt, who relates them here: "While they were in the process of doing some restoration, the old manager could hear laughter and muffled conversation coming from the first row of seats on the ground floor," Affeldt says. "Of course, they weren't your typical movie patrons watching the latest box-office hit. The Rialto was closed at the time to the public."

Underneath the stage are catacombs where the theater's dressing rooms had been located. Although the rooms haven't been used in more than 50 years, the old manager could occasionally smell the scent of heavy perfume. It was a flowery kind of fragrance commonly worn in the 1920s.

"He told me that an actress had allegedly committed suicide by hanging herself from the balcony and from time to time he could hear a thumping sound, almost as if someone had fallen from the balcony. When he went to investigate he couldn't find anyone or anything that could have caused that type of a noise."

Legends that have been circulating for years about the Rialto seem to revolve around that balcony. One employee spoke of a stagehand who had hung himself after he realized that the love he felt for an actress was unrequited. After he was found, the rope was cut to release him, of course, but a few nights later, employees found the rope intact. The former actor's spirit had also been seen sitting in one of the seats when only employees were present and the Rialto was closed to the public.

The spirit of a woman has also been spotted in the northeast corner of the balcony where supposedly she had been killed.

A similar story is that of a janitor who hung himself on the stage. The rope was completely removed, but for years would reappear again in the same spot. The custodian's ghost could be seen walking in front of the screen.

Another employee mentioned that when she was the only one in the building she could set an object down and when she came back later, she would find it in a totally different spot.

The audience wouldn't be too happy when the spirits would be in the mood to toy with the film. Although the projectors were always top of the line, film would break in weird spots, often right in the middle of a movie.

With all the restoration that has taken place, the ghosts may have been chased off. But change usually has the opposite effect on ghosts, making them more active. So, keep an eye open for shadows and dangling ropes, and, by all means, don't put anything down. You may never see it again!

Address:	Rialto Theater 115 W. Kinsley Winslow, AZ 86047
Phone:	(928) 289-4100 (The Rialto is scheduled to reopen in October of 2002.)
Hours:	Call for performance times.

Directions: From Phoenix: Take I-17 North to Flagstaff. Take I-40 East to Winslow; take Exit 252 going into Winslow. This is a one-way street that turns into 2nd Street. When you reach Kinsley, make a right. The Rialto will be on the right.

YUMA TERRITORIAL PRISON

DESPERADOES, WHY DON'T YOU COME TO YOUR SENSES?

From 1876 to 1909, this penitentiary housed more than 3,000 prisoners.

In 1907, due to overcrowding at the Yuma location, convicts began building a new prison at Florence, Arizona. The final group of prisoners were shackled together, marched down Prison Hill and transported to the new facility in the fall of 1909. The old prison buildings served as Yuma Union High School classrooms from 1910-1914. During the Depression they were used as a haven for the homeless.

Do some of the convicts who died here choose to remain behind the cell doors even though death has freed them?

The dreaded "dark cell," where prisoners were confined in solitary for some serious infraction of the rules, measured 10 feet by 10 feet. Each convict would be in complete darkness, sometimes chained to a ringbolt, living on only bread and water; scorpions and sidewinders often shared their cells. Whether these varmints slithered into their quarters from the outside or sadistic guards dropped them in to further torture the inmates—as they claimed—will never be known. After serving their time in solitary, some prisoners were sent directly to an insane asylum in Phoenix.

One of the ghosts who remains behind in the "dark cell" has a reputation of poking, pinching and touching, especially those wearing red clothing. Once, while touring the prison, an amateur psychic said the spirit wasn't a disgruntled prisoner at all, but rather that of a little girl. Perhaps her family was one of the many that found themselves homeless during the Depression.

Assistant Park Manager Jesse Torres was in the museum early one morning when he thought a co-worker had called out to him. "Did you get it?" he recalled her to say. "I proceeded to the back office to talk with her," Torres says, "but learned that she was in the Ramada Building, which isn't even close to the museum. In fact, I was the only one in the museum."

Torres continues: "At the far end of the corridor is Cell 14, which was occupied in the early 1900s by John Ryan. Mr. Ryan was not only disliked by the guards but by the convicts as well. At times when I pass No. 14, I find myself shivering because of the coldness. John was found guilty of a 'crime against nature,' which meant he committed rape or another crime of sexual deviation. Before he finished out his sentence, he committed suicide."

Other reports include witnesses "seeing" things "out of the corner" of their eyes; hearing a woman "singing" in the visitor's area; and seeing a spirit named "Johnny," who loves playing with the coins in the cash register.

A staff writer from *Arizona Highways*, wanting to experience what the convicts went through, attempted to spend 48 hours in the "dark cell." She was shackled to the ringbolt with only a jug of water and a loaf of bread. The magazine scribe fell short of her goal by 11 hours. The author of *Haunts of Arizona* did a 13-hour incarceration. He reported dazzling white shapes floating around in the pitch darkness of his cell.

Address:	Yuma Territorial Prison State Historic Park 1 Prison Hill Road Yuma, AZ 85364
Phone:	(928) 783-4771
Hours:	8 a.m.-5 p.m., daily except Christmas
Directions:	From Phoenix: Take I-10 West to Exit 112 (SR85). Travel SR85 south to Gila Bend; drive through town and get on I-8 West, to Yuma. Take Giss Parkway Exit—Turn left at stop sign. Go to the first street on the right before the underpass (Prison Hill Road).

BIBLIOGRAPHY

BOOKS

Cline, Platt.
   Mountain Town: Flagstaff's First Century, Flagstaff: Northland Press, 1994.

Botts, Gene with John and Marge Osborne.
   The Vulture, Phoenix: Quest Publishing Group, 1995.

Cockrum, E. Lendell and Maierhauser, M. K.
   The TIMELINE: The Intertwined Histories of Colossal Cave and La
   Posta *Quemada Ranch*, Vail: Colossal Cave Mountain Park 1996.

Eppinga, Jane.
   Arizona Twilight Tales, Boulder: Pruett Publishing Company, 2000.

Gill, Sharon A. and Dave R. Oester.
   The Haunted Reality, St. Helens, OR: StarWest Images, 1996.

Grossman, Carolyn and Myal, Suzanne.
   Discovering Tucson, Tucson: Fiesta Publishing, 1996.

Haak, Wilbur A.
   Globe's Historic Buildings, Globe: Gila Cty. Hist. Society, 1998.

Kiefer, D.R.
   Haunts of Arizona, Mesa: Shadow Publishing, 2000.

Martin, Judy.
   Arizona Walls, Phoenix: Double B Publications, 1997.

McBride, Dennis.
   Midnight on Arizona Street: The Secret Life of the Boulder Dam Hotel, Boulder City: Boulder City/Hoover Dam Museum 1993.

Mulford, Karen Surina.
   Arizona's Historic Escapes, Winston-Salem: John F. Blair, Publisher, 1997.

Mulford, Karen Surina.
   Arizona's Historic Restaurants, Winston-Salem: John F. Blair, Publisher,
   1995.

Pierce, Dale.
   Wild West Characters, Phoenix: American Traveler Press, 1991.

Summerhayes, Martha.
   Vanished Arizona, University of Nebraska Press, 1979.

Trimble, Marshall.
   Roadside History of Arizona, Missoula: Mountain Press Publishing Co.,
   1986.

Young, Herbert V.
   They Came to Jerome-The Billion Dollar Copper Camp, Jerome: The Jerome Historical Society, 1972.

Weir, Bill.
   Arizona Traveler's Handbook, Chico: Moon Publications, 1987.

Wilson, Bruce M.
   Crown King and the Southern Bradshaws: A Complete History. Mesa: Crown King Press, 1990.

Wood, Ted.
   Ghosts of the Southwest, New York: Walker and Company, 1997.

ARTICLES

Carroll, Tony. "Rumors haunt old Yuma prison," *Arizona Republic* 11/21/99.

Hill, Tex. "The angel who haunts Tombstone," *Examiner*, 11/6/84.

Lowe, Sam. "Couple slowly revive turn-of-the-century hotel," *Arizona Republic* 4/19/99.

Negri, Sam. "Renovation revives Tucson hotel's quiet elegance," *Arizona Republic* 9/20/85.

Taylor, Marilyn. "37 Hours Of Terror In The Dark Cell," *Arizona Highways* 2/95.

VIDEOS

The History Channel, *Haunted Nevada*, A & E. Television Networks: New York: New Video Group.

Chamber of Commerce Phone Numbers

Bisbee	866-224-7233	Kingman	928-753-6253
Camp Verde	928-567-9294	Mesa	480-969-1307
Casa Grande	800-916-1515	Phoenix	602-254-5521
Cottonwood	928-634-7593	Pinetop	800-573-4031
Crown King Saloon	928-632-7053	Prescott	800-266-7534
Douglas	520-364-2477	Sierra Vista	520-458-6940
Eagar	928-333-2123	Tempe	480-967-7891
Ehrenberg	928-923-9661	Tombstone	520-457-9317
Flagstaff	800-842-7293	Tubac	520-398-2704
Florence	800-437-9433	Tucson	520-792-1212
Globe	800-804-5623	Wickenburg	928-684-5479
Greer	928-333-2123	Willcox	520-384-2272
Hoover Dam	702-293-2034	Williams	928-635-4061
Humboldt	928-632-4355	Winslow	928-289-2434
Jerome	928-634-2900	Yuma	928-782-2567

ABOUT THE AUTHOR

Ellen Robson was raised in Springfield, IL and has lived in the Phoenix area since 1969. She now lives in Tempe with her husband, John, and spends much of her time with their children and grandchildren.

Ellen also coauthored *Haunted Highway: The Spirits of Route 66*. When she isn't writing books about haunted sites, she freelances for various publications including *Woman's World* and *Arizona Senior World*.

Ellen invites you to share any other ghost "sites" that you know of in Arizona that you would like to see included in future books. Her address is P.O. Box 27282, Tempe, AZ 85285 or you can visit her website at: http://www.spirits66.com

ACKNOWLEDGMENTS

Special thanks to:

The contributors who were willing to share the history of their buildings as well as their personal experiences with their resident ghosts.

John who was there for me 100%, traveling all those extra miles for "just one more story," proofreading, encouragement and gentle push for me to finish.

Dad for accompanying us on so many of our jaunts looking for another haunted restaurant or hotel.

Eric, Cathi and Renee, my family in Illinois and my cherished friends for their love and loyal support.

Rebeca, for her computer skills and help in finding the perfect title.

Golden West Publishers for taking a chance with my first book, *Haunted Highway-The Spirits of Route 66*.

And Trudi, who never has time to get away for lunch but still made time for my endless phone calls.

INDEX

Adobe Oven Bakery 73
Affeldt, Allan 123
Alaniz, Shulamite 65
Alexandria 21
animals
    cat, Morris 10
    dog, Mona 35
Angel of Tombstone 92
Arizona Biltmore Hotel 64
Arizona Highways 126
Arizona Hotel, Prescott 78
Arizona Republic, The 89
Aunt Chilada's at Squaw Peak 64, 66
Babcock, Jeannene 11
Baker, Jennifer 10
Balaam, Frank 39
Barela, Mark 44
Barrows Boarding House 94
Bast, Mary & Charlie 46
Behringer, Lynne 71
Bell, Shawn 101
Bisbee 9, 11
Bo Jo's Grill & Sports Club 121-122
Boulder Canyon Project Act 48
Boulder City/Hoover Dam Museum 50
Bouvier, Leon 71
Bradshaw Mountains 22
Brawley, Hank & Bessie 25
Brekhus, Robin 23
British ladies 73
Bruchman's Trading Post 121
Buckley, Juanita 67
Burbank, Michael 33
Butterfield Express 100
Café Espress 31
Camelback Inn 64
Camp Verde 12-13
Carrillo, Enrique & Lupe 15
Casa Grande 7, 15-17
Casa Grande Café 14-15
Casey Moore's Oyster House 86-87
Charlie Clark's Steak House 77
Chiricahua Mountains 111
clairvoyant 65
Clanton, Billy 94

Clark, Charlie 76
Clark, Russell 98
Clossen, Edmond, Fr 82
Coca-Cola Plant 44
Cobre Valley Center for the Arts 38, 41
Colorado River 48
Colossal Cave 104, 106
Conlin, Ann 55
Conlin, David & Sandy 55
Connor, Dave 54
Connor Hotel 54, 56
Copper Cities Community Players 41
Cottonwood 20
Cottonwood Hotel 18, 20
Coyote Joe's Bar & Grill 78-79
Crowe, Frank T. 48
Crown King 21-22
Crown King Saloon & Restaurant 21-22
Crystal Magic 32-33
Daisy Mae's Stronghold 84-85
dark cell 125
Davis, Sallie Calvert 88
de Otero, Don Toribio 96
Dobson-Hunt, Kate 113
Douglas 8, 24
Drake, Jodi 83
Dreamy Draw 64
Eagar 25, 27
Ehrenberg 8, 29
Ehrenberg Cemetery 29
Ellis, Don & Candy 62
Erickson, Neil & Emma 110
Ethington, Mrs. 16
Ethington, Peter 16
exorcism 15
Faraway Ranch 110-111
Fat Cat Cookies 8
Faulkner, Randy 83
Flagstaff 31, 33, 35
Flagstaff Theatre 30
Florence 37, 125
Famous People
    Allen, Rex 112
    Dillinger, John 98
    Earp, Wyatt 34

Elvis   18
Grey, Zane   34
Hearst, William Randolph   34
Langtry, Lily   69
Martha Summerhayes   28
Noel Coward   83
Roosevelt, Teddy, President   34
Sellecks, Tom   24
Wayne, John   18, 90
West, Mae   18
Fort Verde State Historic Park   12-13
Fray Marcos Hotel and Depot   119
Gadsden Hotel   8, 23-24
Gallagher, Vicki   28
Gastineau, Lou   25
Ghostly Occurrences
a cold presence covering his body   55
a gambler   23
apparition   8, 10
army-style khaki clothing   24
billowing smoke   79
bizarre ghost   16
bride and groom ghosts   35
choking sensation   15
cigar aroma   121
clunking sound   12
cold spots   11
dancing couples   52
energy vortex   56
flickering candles   13
foul odor   29
ghost   17
ghost in black   23
guardian spirits   49
hanging rope   124
headless   24
heavy footsteps   12
heavy perfume   123
heavy presence   17
hovering and glistening   11
Indian maiden   106
Lady in White   17
lady wearing white   33
light brush   13
little boy   8, 96
little girl   29, 61, 68, 126
luminescent balls of light   29

missing hammers   58
old man   14
old miner   33
pinching waitresses bottoms   51
presences   49
protective spirits   11
red flannel shirt   29
shadow   11
shimmering light   10
shiny black suit   24
small boy   11
small children   26
sobbing   43
spirit   14
spirit energy   29
spirit photograph   19-20
The Lady in White   16
three noisy little boys   70
tweaking your toes   9
unmistakable odor   17
whistling   120
women whispering   55
Ghost of Tubac   97
Ghost Room   84
ghost town   107
Gibson, Bill & Tricia   76
Gila County sheriff   42
Glendale   7
Globe   41-45
Ghosts by Name
Abe Lincoln   69
Aunt Genieva   25
Charlie   84
Charlie Clark   77
Clara   120
Emma Erickson   111
Eve   114, 116
Faith   80
Father Michael   82
Frank "Pops" Schmidt   104
George   100
George Brooks   18
Ghost of Tubac   97
Grandpa Bruchman   121
Hugo, a Viet Nam veteran   21
Jeannie   43
Jensen, Leone   8

Johnny   96, 126
Jonathon   24
Lady in White   104
Leatherbelly   21
Leonard Monti   91
Leone Jensen   70
Mary Moeur   86
Mitt Wiltbank   27
Mr. Shelby   51
Nellie   93
Resurrection Mary   69
Rod Graves   118
Sara Winchester   69
Skeeter   37
Slim   67
T.S.   98
Vince   99
Gods of Wisdom   69
Grand Canyon   119
Grand Canyon Railway   119
Graves, Rodney & Helen   117
Greene, Bob   52
Greer   7, 47
Guedon, Gerald & Jessie   60
gunfight at the O.K. Corral   94
hanging tree   108
Harvey, Fred   119
Harvey Girls   119
Hassayampa Inn   7, 80-81
Haunted Hamburger   57-58
Haunts of Arizona   126
Hayden, Charles   88
Hayden Hotel   88
Hayden, Sallie & Mary   88
Hayden, Senator Carl   88
Heritage Square   71
Herndon, Stephen   31
Holst, John   114
Hoover Dam   48
Horton, Fay   17
Hotel Brunswick   59, 61
Hotel Congress   98, 99
Hotel San Carlos   8, 69-70
Hotel Weatherford   34
Humboldt   51, 53
Hunting, Russ   109
Inn at Castle Rock   9, 11

Jackson, Michael   16
Jacobs, Jeannie   121
Jake Renfro's Famous Log Cabin Café   76
Jerome   54, 56, 58
Johnny's Country Corner   44-45
Johnson's Grocery Store   14
Jurisin, Eric & Michelle   57
Kennedy, Patrice   102
Kiefer, Don   106
King of Spain   96
Kingman   60-61
ladies of the night   21
Landmark Restaurant   63
Leff, Karen   18
Li'l Abner's Steakhouse   100-101
Martha Summerhayes   8
Martinez, Jesus   36
Matthews, Maureen   86
McBride, Dennis   49
McCright, W. D.   61
Melikian, Greg   69
Mesa   63
Moeur   86
Moeur, Wm. & Mary   86
Monti, Leonard   89
Monti's La Casa Vieja   89, 91
Mule Mountains   9
Munson, Bob   12
Nagel, Candice & Ken   64
Native American spiritualist   53
Native Americans   69
Neilsen, Kathrine   111
Nellie Cashman's Restaurant   92-93
Ninth & Ash Restaurant   86
Oester, Sharon & Dave   56
Old Gila County Jail   43
Oro Belle   21
Osborne, John & Marge   108
Oseran, Richard & Shana   98
Payson   7
Peek Steakhouse   64
Peoria   7
Phoenix   7, 55, 66, 69-70, 72, 75
Phoenix insane asylum   125
Pinetop   77
Pioneer Arizona Living History
    Museum   68

Pointe at Squaw Peak   64
Prescott   7, 68, 81-83, 88
Prescott Fine Arts Association   7, 82-83
professional spirit photographers   56
psychic   11, 18, 27, 49-50, 108, 126
Pullman coach car   119
Quetu, Alfred, Fr.   82
Red Garter Bed and Bakery   116
Revak, Joe   14
Rex Allen Museum/Willcox Cowboy
      Hall of Fame   112-113
Rialto Theatre   123-124
Riata Pass Gallery   52-53
Riata Pass Steakhouse   51
Richard, Daniel & Romelle   25
Riggs, Ed & Lillian   110
Rodriguez, Christine   11
Rod's Steak House   118
Route 66   114, 117
Russ House   92
Ryan, Cathy   30
Ryan, Jan   111
Ryan, John   126
Sacred Heart Catholic Church   92
Sacred Heart Church   82
sacred water   69
Salt River   88
Sanchez, Lawrence & Stella   117
Schley Saloon   112
Schneider, Linda   73
Schwertner, Josef   112
Sierra Vista   84-85
Skinner, Anita   92
Skinner, Sherri   92
14Sophia's
spirit photography   29
Spirit Room Bar   56
spiritualist   18
St. Vincent, Patty   86
Stables Restaurant and Lounge   96
Stroub, Robert   11
Taylor, Eddie   36
Taylor, Henry   34
Taylor's Bed and Breakfast   37
Teague, Connie   42
Teeter, Eliza   71
Teeter House   71-72

Tempe   87, 88, 91
The Property Conference Center   17
Tobin, Mary   119
Tombstone   92-95
Tombstone Boarding House   94-95
Torres, Jesse   126
town too tough to die   92
Trejo, Alberto   116
True Detective Magazine   98
Tubac   96, 97
Tubac Golf Resort   97
Tucson   98-99, 101, 103
University of Arizona's Centennial
      Hall   102-103
Vail   106
Vail, James   32
Valley of the Sun   90
Valley Youth Theater   75
Victorian   7-9, 11, 64, 68, 74, 93, 95, 99
Victorian Tea Room   71
Viet Nam veteran   21
Villarin, Ted & Shirley   94
Vintage Hideaway   25
Visor, Robert   11
Vulture City   107, 109
Vulture Mine   107
Webb, Del   73
White Mountain Lodge   47
Wickenburg   109
Wickenburg, Henry   107
Willcox   111, 113
Willcox Cowboy Hall of Fame   112
Willcox, Don   84
Williams   7, 116, 118, 120
Williams Depot   119-120
Wiltbank, Genieva & Milford (Mitt)   25
Winslow   122-124
Yuma   126
Yuma Territorial Prison   125-126

Haunted Highway
The Spirits of Route 66

Sixty-six spine-tingling tales of haunted homes, businesses and graveyards along America's "Mother Road." From the *Biograph Theater* in Chicago to the *Pointe Vincente Lighthouse* on the Pacific Coast, these fascinating accounts of ghostly activities will provide you with hours of reading enjoyment. By Ellen Robson and Dianne Halicki.5 1/2 x 8 1/2 — 136 pages . . . $12.95

Sleeping With Ghosts

Ghostly encounters of the Arizona kind! Tour Arizona's haunted hotels, inns and bed and breakfasts. Join paranormal investigator, Debbie Branning, as she relates legends and her personal experiences at Arizona's most haunted accommodations!

5 1/2 x 8 1/2 — 152 Pages . . . $12.95

Easy RV Recipes

Author Ferne Holmes brings you her favorite recipes to make in your RV, camper or houseboat. Utensils, supplies, food and daily menus. Social campfire cooking section!

5 1/2 x 8 1/2 — 128 Pages . . . $9.95

Western Breakfast & Brunch Recipes

A roundup of hearty Western favorites to start your day! Includes ranch-style recipes, Native American and gourmet recipes. Add a western flair to your traditional morning meal!

5 1/2 x 8 1/2 — 96 Pages . . . $9.95

Grandma's Favorite Country Recipes

From grits and sausage to roasts and ribs, from breads and muffins to soups and stews–our universal Grandma is represented throughout the recipes. Illustrated by award-winning artist Debbie Bell Jarratt. Compiled by Michael J. Liddy and a lot of grandkids.

8 1/2 x 8 1/2 - 160 Pages . . . $14.95

Arizona Cookbook

INDIAN
MEXICAN
WESTERN
ARIZONA PRODUCTS
BACKPACKING-CAMPING
PATIO-BARBECUE

A COLLECTION OF MORE THAN 250 AUTHENTIC ARIZONA RECIPES

REVISED EDITION

California COOK BOOK

Capturing that classic California flavor!

Recipes reflecting the fusion of flavors from
the Pacific Rim to South of the Border.

ILLINOIS Cook Book

Savor the flavors of Illinois,
from the tastes of Chicago to the wildflower prairies!

KANSAS COOK BOOK

MISSOURI COOK BOOK

◊ Tempting Appetizers   ◊ Soups & Salads
◊ Hearty Breakfasts   ◊ Delicious Entrees
◊ Savory Side Dishes   ◊ Delightful Desserts
◊ Heritage Specialties   ◊ Breads
◊ Barbecue Recipes   ◊ Trivia

New Mexico Cookbook

175 Recipes from the "Land of Enchantment"

Indian Recipes, Old Mexico Recipes, Salsa Recipes,
Tortilla Recipes, and Chile Recipes
The best of New Mexico cooking!

OKLAHOMA COOK BOOK

Featuring Sooner/Boomer Frontier Favorites!

TEXAS COOK BOOK

★ BARBECUE   ★ CHILI
★ TEX-MEX   ★ SEAFOOD
★ CREOLE   ★ COWBOY

Tons of Tasty Texas
Recipes with Terrific
Texas Trivia Too!

All state cookbooks are $9.95. To order, call (800) 521-9221 or
visit www.AmericanTravelerPress.com

ORDER BLANK

AMERICAN TRAVELER PRESS

☼ **5738 North Central Avenue • Phoenix, AZ 85012**

www.americantravelerpress.com • 1-800-521-9221 • FAX 602-234-3062

Qty	Title	Price	Amount
	Arizona Adventure	9.95	
	Arizona Cookbook	9.95	
	Arizona Legends and Lore	9.95	
	Arizona Territory Cookbook	9.95	
	Arizona Trails and Tales	14.95	
	Arizoniana	9.95	
	Arrows, Bullets and Saddle Sores	9.95	
	Billy the Kid Cookbook	9.95	
	Cowboy Slang	9.95	
	Days of the West	14.95	
	Desert Survival Handbook	8.95	
	Discover Arizona!	6.95	
	Experience Jerome	6.95	
	Finding Gold in the Desert	5.95	
	Ghost Towns and Historical Haunts in Arizona	12.95	
	Haunted Arizona	12.95	
	Hiking Arizona	6.95	
	In Old Arizona	9.95	
	Mavericks—Ten Uncorralled Westerners	5.00	
	Old West Adventures in Arizona	9.95	
	Prehistoric Arizona	5.00	
	Tales of Arizona Territory	14.95	
	Wild West Heroes & Rogues: Wyatt Earp	6.95	

U.S. Shipping & Handling Add:
(Shipping to all other countries see website.)

1-3 Books $3.00
4+ Books $5.00

Arizona residents add 9.3% sales tax

Total $_____
(Payable in U.S. funds)

☐ My Check or Money Order Enclosed

☐ MasterCard ☐ VISA ☐ AMEX ☐ Discover   Verification code_____

Acct. No. _____ Exp. Date _____

Signature _____

Name _____ Phone _____

Address _____

City/State/Zip _____

Call for a FREE catalog of all our titles — Prices subject to change —